Consciousness in Advaita Vedānta

William M. Indich

MOTILAL BANARSIDASS PUBLISHERS
PRIVATE LIMITED • DELHI

First Edition: Delhi, 1980
Reprint: Delhi, 1995, 2000

ISBN: 81-208-1251-4

Also available at:
MOTILAL BANARSIDASS
236, 9th Main III Block, Jayanagar, Bangalore 560 011
41 U.A. Bungalow Road, Jawahar Nagar, Delhi 110 007
8 Mahalaxmi Chamber, Warden Road, Mumbai 400 026
120 Royapettah High Road, Mylapore, Chennai 600 004
Sanas Plaza, 1302 Baji Rao Road, Pune 411 002
8 Camac Street, Calcutta 700 017
Ashok Rajpath, Patna 800 004
Chowk, Varanasi 221 001

Printed in India
BY JAINENDRA PRAKASH JAIN AT SHRI JAINENDRA PRESS,
A-45 NARAINA, PHASE-I, NEW DELHI 110 028
AND PUBLISHED BY NARENDRA PRAKASH JAIN FOR
MOTILAL BANARSIDASS PUBLISHERS PRIVATE LIMITED,
BUNGALOW ROAD, DELHI 110 007

To
My Father and Mother

PREFACE

Philosophers have often argued that theirs is a reflective discipline, one which emerges as man begins to question what has been accepted uncritically as the basis of the universe and human experience. Sooner or later, however, another thought arises. "All this time," someone reasons, "I have been thinking about many things without questioning the nature of the intelligence upon which my assumptions and reflections depend." Stated more generally, we have been thinking without reflecting upon the nature of reflection itself. What is the nature of human awareness ? Whence does it emerge ? Is consciousness human or divine, finite or infinite ? Philosophers, religious thinkers and scientists East and West have long tried to answer these and related questions, and today, of course, interest in the nature of consciousness is as vital as ever. Increasingly sophisticated scientific instruments have provided vast quantities of new data in terms of which neurophysiologists and psychologists are "mapping" the structure of the brain. A great deal of attention is being paid to behavioral abnormalities and learning disabilities in order to discover what factors might twist or inhibit the development of socially adjusted and conventionally productive consciousness. And many behaviorally oriented philosophers have been trying to analyze states of human consciousness in terms of action, or the intentions and desires which motivate action.

But other psychologists, theologians and philosophers have rejected the attempted "objectification" of consciousness, arguing instead that consciousness can neither be reduced to matter nor fully understood by observation alone. And many of the thinkers who have voiced this view in the West have drawn both inspiration and confirmation from various Asian theories of consciousness. This book focuses on one such theory, the nature of consciousness according to Advaita Vedānta. For Advaita Vedānta, the most influential school of classical Indian thought and the most well-known system of Indian thought, along with Yoga, in the West, the study of consciousness is the study of human awareness. But human awareness is not exhausted in ordinary perception, knowledge and experience. For Advaita, human awareness also encompasses transcendental consciousness, or the realization of the identity of human consciousness with all existence, intelligence and value in the universe. As a result of this mystical, non-dualistic vision, the study of the Advaitic theory of consciousness amounts to an exposition of the heart of the Advaitic philosophical system, including a description of non-dual reality and human freedom as well as the varieties of dualistic awareness; waking, dream and deep sleep.

Because consciousness is so central to Advaitic thought, we have come to expect both Indian and Western studies of Advaitic metaphysics, epistemology and logic to devote a good deal of attention elaborating the identification of Self with reality and the relationship between reality and the illusory world of phenomenal experience. See, for example, works by K. C. Bhattacharyya, T. M. P. Mahadevan, P. Deussen and E. Deutsch. In contrast with the present work, however, none of these studies has focused attention exclusively and systematically on consciousness itself. And among books dealing with consciousness in Indian philosophy, e.g., those by S. K. Saksena and J.Chethimattam, none has offered a systematic, critical analysis of the Advaitic theory of consciousness. Finally, studies by J. F. Staal, R. Guenon, R. Otto and others have opened the door to the vast and relatively new field of comparative philosophy while leaving much room for others, like myself, to contribute additional material. Thus, this book is a systematic, critical and comparative treatment of the Advaitic theory of consciousness, and one which will hopefully prove valuable to students of Indian philosophy as well as to a broader audience interested in the perennial question of the nature of human awareness.

This book is a revision of a doctoral dissertation in comparative philosophy completed at the University of Hawaii in 1978. I wish to express my sincere thanks to Professor Eliot Deutsch, whose seminar on Consciousness provided both the inspiration and the starting point for the present study, to Dr Frederic L. Bender, whose academic assistance has been surpassed only by his constant friendship, and to Professor Winfield E. Nagley, who extended himself on my behalf without hesitation more than once. Finally, to Professor K. N. Upadhyaya, I offer my deepest gratitude and respect, for without his continued concern, there can be no doubt that this work would never have been initiated, let alone completed.

And to Susan, no amount of thanks is enough.

CONTENTS

CHAPTER I

INTRODUCTION : AN OVERVIEW OF THE ADVAITIC SYSTEM

This chapter serves two purposes. The first is to provide a brief introduction to the general philosophical system of Advaita Vedānta. The second is to present an overview of the Advaitic theory of consciousness and to indicate its place in Advaitic thought.

The Philosophy of Advaita

Classical orthodox Indian philosophy is traditionally discussed in terms of six major schools,[1] most of which spawned over time a rich variety of sub-schools that differed from each other according to their exposition and defense of the basic doctrines upheld by their parent systems. Each of the six major systems was known as a *darśana,* a term derived from the Sanskrit verbal root, *dṛś,* meaning "to see" and conveying in this context the sense of a vision of truth or a direct, immediate insight into the nature of reality. It would not be an exaggeration to say that one of these visions, the Vedānta or Uttara Mīmāṁsā,[2] has succeeded in capturing the Indian intellectual and religious imagination to such an extent that this vision has played a predominant role in Indian thought since its initial systematic exposition along non-dualistic or Advaitic lines by Śaṅkara (ca. 788-820). Clearly, a thinker, whether he be a secular visionary or religious saint, cannot capture the spirit of a culture to the degree that Śaṅkara did by merely manufacturing or inventing a system of thought based solely on his individual

---

1. The six classical schools, traditionally grouped in three pairs, are : Nyāya-Vaiśeṣika; Sāṅkhya-Yoga; Pūrva Mīmāṁsā-Vedānta.

2. Vedānta means the culmination of Vedic wisdom, both historically and philosophically. It is also called Uttara Mīmāṁsā, which means later systematization, following the earlier Pūrva Mīmāṁsā of Vedic ritualism. There are different sub-schools of Vedānta, such as : Dvaita of Madhva; Dvaitādvaita of Nimbārka; Viśiṣṭādvaita of Rāmānuja; Advaita of Śaṅkara, etc.

understanding. Rather, a philosopher such as Śaṅkara succeeds in providing a culture with a good portion of its intellectual inspiration by tapping into some of the basic and vitally important traditions which nourish that culture and which provide it with its distinctive, as well as universal, components.

The heritage from which Śaṅkara synthesizes and systematizes the Advaita Vedānta philosophy is known as the Triple Foundation of Vedānta (*prasthāna-traya*), consisting of the *Upaniṣads*, the *Bhagavad Gītā* and the *Vedānta*, or *Brahma Sūtra*. However, we would be mistaken if we were to think that Śaṅkara's philosophy is nothing more than a literal commentary on this literature. One has only to look, for example, at the way Śaṅkara is put upon to incorporate many of the theistic, devotional and action oriented stanzas of the *Bhagavad Gītā* into his non-dualistic and knowledge oriented philosophy to see that he is an interpreter of most sophisticated skill and subtlety whose prime concern is the exposition of a particular and in many ways quite unconventional vision.[1]

Rather than merely offering a commentary then, Śaṅkara uses these traditional texts as the authoritative scriptural basis from which his elaboration of a vision of non-dual, transcendental and purely spiritual reality (Brahman, Ātman) follows. For this reason, Śaṅkara's philosophical system focuses primary attention on scriptural discussions of transcendental reality rather than on logic, cosmology, ritualism or psychology, with which the traditional texts also deal and which became objects of primary concern for the other orthodox systems of thought. Indeed, it was precisely in their claim that transcendental, non-dual consciousness is the essence of both the subjective and objective elements of our experience and of ultimate reality itself that Śaṅkara, and the Advaitins following him, succeeded in articulating the essence of the Indian understanding of both the meaning of human life and the nature of the universe.

But the Advaitic vision did not altogether undermine the attempts of Indian intellectuals to come to terms with empirical issues. For Śaṅkara, who was one of Hinduism's greatest religious reformers, lived at a time when the influence of Indian Buddhism had begun to wane but before the orthodox tradition

1. J. F. Staal, *Advaita and Neoplatonism*, p. 134.

had found a unifying direction. Thus the image of Śaṅkara stuck away in some cave dwelling on his non-dual vision could not be further from fact; at least according to traditional biographical accounts Śaṅkara travelled to the four corners of the Indian sub-continent establishing monasteries and providing fresh spiritual direction for Hindu culture.[1] And as part of this new direction, Śaṅkara established a particular intellectual framework which allowed for the reconciliation of conflicting philosophical views. While empirical concerns such as logic or cosmology, ritual or psychology were understood in the context of Śaṅkara's new spiritual direction as both unnecessary and inappropriate for the attainment of man's highest good, the realization of ultimate reality itself, they were nevertheless granted relative efficacy and value and were thus incorporated into the Advaitic vision of the varieties of human experience and valid knowledge. In a similar vein, post-Śaṅkara Advaitins never challenged the validity of Śaṅkara's vision of ultimate reality, although they did disagree with each other regarding the specific logical, cosmological and psychological details involved in the elaboration of that vision. More of the conciliatory and synthetic dimensions of Śaṅkara's thought will be discussed at the end of this chapter. Now, however, we turn our attention to a general outline of the philosophy of Advaita.

What is the Advaitic vision of reality ? The heart of Advaitic thinking can be summarized in three concise statements : Brahman is non-dual and unchanging reality; the world is illusion; man's eternal Self (Ātman) is not different from reality (Brahman).[2] The Advaitic system of thought is one of impressive philosophical economy, which is to say that Advaitic metaphysics, epistemology, ethics and axiology are variations upon the common theme of the reality of non-dual Brahman. In other words, the point of departure for each of these philosophical fields is unitary Brahman and the central principle upheld throughout the elaboration of each part of the whole system is the non-duality of Brahman. However, one should be cautioned against treating Advaita as a variety of monism if, by this label, one wishes to refer to a philosophical theory which maintains that all plurality or

1. Cf. Swāmī Nikhilānanda, *Self-Knowledge*, pp. ix-xi.

2. Cf. the frequently repeated verse : *Brahma satyam jagan mithyā jīvo Brahmaiva nāparaḥ.*

multiplicity can be explained in terms of one principle of objective being. Advaitins are quick to point out that, contrary to such a monistic position, the reality they uphold "does not require variety or multiplicity ... in order to be affirmed."[1]

Let us first look at Advaitic metaphysics with the point of philosophical unity in mind. The *Upaniṣads* repeat numerous times and in numerous ways that "verily, all this is Brahman."[2] This statement does not aim at establishing an identity between the phenomenal (*vyāvahārika*) world of appearance and ultimate (*pāramārthika*) reality of Brahman. Rather, it aims at showing that the world which appears to be real in ordinary experience is, in fact, completely dependent for its being on Brahman. But this dependence moves in one direction only, i.e., Brahman in no way depends on the world for its existence. Further, this total dependence extends to all intelligence and value in the universe; they too are derived ultimately from Brahman. Thus Brahman is characterized by Śaṅkara as existence, consciousness and bliss (*saccidānanda*). Brahman is the ground (*adhiṣṭhāna*) of all creation, the consciousness presupposed by all knowing and the object which is eternally desirable in and for itself. To prevent the designations existence, consciousness and bliss from seeming to limit Brahman, however, Advaitins specify that these words do not refer to parts, attributes or accidents of reality but that they actually constitute its unitary and essential nature (*svarūpa*). In other words, "existence is consciousness, and consciousness is bliss."[3]

But Śaṅkara states that words used to define Brahman actually function "to differentiate Brahman from other entities that possess opposite qualities."[4] Thus, it is only in order to distinguish Brahman from the world, and to offer a description of man's experience of reality, that Brahman is "said to be existence, consciousness and bliss. In Brahman's essential nature, however, there is no split, and no distinction."[5] Advaitins have clarified

1. Eliot Deutsch, *Advaita Vedānta*, p. 3.

2. *Chāndogya Upaniṣad* 3.14.1. (*Sarvam idam Brahma eva*). Cf. *Maitri Upaniṣad* 4.6., *Bṛhadāraṇyaka Upaniṣad* 2.4.6., 3.4.1.

3. T. M. P. Mahadevan, *The Pañcadaśī*, pp. xxiv-xxv; Deutsch, *op. cit.*, p. 9.

4. *Taittirīya Upaniṣad Śaṅkara Bhāṣya* 2.1.1., quoted in Deutsch, *op. cit.*, p. 11.

5. Mahadevan, *op. cit.*, p. xxv.

their understanding of the provisional nature of this definition by calling it a definition depicting the essential character (*svarūpa-lakṣaṇa*) of Brahman, one which offers a description of the essence of Brahman realization. In no sense does this essential definition qualify or limit reality in the way that an ultimate ontological definition, or the attempt to qualify Brahman conceptually, would. The *Upaniṣads* make this same point through the use of the well-known *via negativa*, reality is "not this, not that" (*neti, neti*).[1] Since all phenomenal distinctions depend on Brahman, they cannot serve as adequate means to apprehend or define it. Thus the utter non-duality is upheld, but at the cost, which to some would undoubtedly seem too high, of making reality unthinkable (*acintya*) and indescribable (*anirvacanīya*).

How is it that eternal, unchanging Brahman is the ground of impermanent, phenomenal appearance ? What is the relationship between Brahman and the world ? The Advaitic response to these questions involves us in the introduction of the concept of *māyā* and the distinction between levels or degrees of reality. *Māyā* is said to be the power by which Brahman is concealed and by which a distortion, in the form of the apparent world, takes place. Advaitins personify Brahman along with its creative power, *māyā*, as Īśvara, the Lord, whose joyous, sportive and spontaneous activity accounts for the appearance of the phenomenal world. Īśvara is the efficient and material cause of *māyā* which, as the concealment and distortion of Brahman, is less real than Brahman itself. Yet the created world, with its myriad of practical effects, cannot be said to be unreal, i.e., that which "can never be a content of experience."[2] Indeed, Īśvara's cosmic illusion certainly seems real enough to those who are subject to it, and rightly so according to the Advaitic perspective, since *māyā* defines the limits within which our phenomenal experience is confined. In this sense, *māyā* is indescribable with respect to reality or unreality (*sadasadanirvacanīyam*).

One important implication of this position is that it only makes sense to ask about the nature of the relationship between Brahman and the world, that is, to ask how Brahman causes the world, from within the limits of the world. No causal or any

1. *Bṛhadāraṇyaka Upaniṣad* 3.9.26 ; 4.2.4.; 4.4.22.
2. Deutsch, *op. cit.*, p. 25.

other sort of relationship pertains to Brahman in itself because at this highest level of reality there is nothing else. In other words, Advaitic philosophy draws a radical ontological distinction between Brahman and the world, and between the world and unreality. The world appears to emerge from Brahman only from within the context of the world. But from the ultimate standpoint of Brahman, there is no world. With plurality thus relegated to the level of appearance, the utter non-duality of reality is upheld.

Advaitic epistemology is grounded in and follows consistently from its metaphysical position. Śaṅkara presents the epistemological correlate of the ontological distinction between Brahman and the world by referring to the Upaniṣadic passage which states that "There are two kinds of knowledge (*vidyā*) to be attained, the higher (*parā*) and the lower (*aparā*)."[1] The text elaborates this distinction in terms of the difference between the knowledge by which the immutable, everlasting, all-pervading and imperishable, i.e., Brahman, is realized, and the "knowledge of the world — of objects, events, means, ends, virtues and vices."[2] Thus higher knowledge is knowledge of reality, while lower knowledge has as its object the created world, phenomenal appearance. That these two kinds of knowledge are as radically different as the levels of reality to which they correspond is further confirmed by the Advaitic analysis of the nature of knowledge. Knowledge of the lower kind participates in the causal order and has moral consequence (*karman*). This kind of knowledge results from an activity or process involving the knower (*pramātā*), the object of knowledge (*prameya*) and the instrument or means of knowledge (*pramāṇa*). By contrast, higher knowledge is neither an effect nor a cause of anything, is beyond karmic consequence and transmigratory existence (*saṁsāra*) and does not involve the subject-object duality of lower knowledge. Rather, higher knowledge is a fully autonomous state of being in which the identity of the all-pervading consciousness underlying the apparently distinct subject, object and means of knowledge is realized.

Thus, for the Advaitin, higher knowledge is strictly speaking

1. *Muṇḍaka Upaniṣad* 1.1.4., quoted in Deutsch, *op. cit.*, p. 81.
2. *Ibid.*, p. 82.

not subjective knowledge *of* reality as object. Instead it is the awareness of the identity of the knowing subject with reality itself. In other words, in higher knowledge the essence of the knowing subject is realized to be identical with the essence of the objective world. Here knowledge and reality, epistemology and metaphysics merge in non-duality. When the essence of the knowing subject, the Self (Ātman) is known, all reality is known. "That which is the finest essence — this whole world has that as its soul. That is Reality. That is Ātman. Thou art that."[1] But if the essence of the subject, Ātman, is identical with reality, how is it that we are ignorant of this identity ?

Advaitins treat the ignorance (*avidyā*) of the identity of Self and Brahman as a process which functions according to a mechanism known as superimposition (*adhyāsa*). In its most general application, superimposition is defined by Śaṅkara as "the apparent presentation to consciousness, in the form of remembrance, of something previously observed in some other thing."[2] In this form, the notion of superimposition is used by Advaitins to explain the notion of error or falsity. For example, a rope, which is immediately present to consciousness, appears to be a snake because we superimpose the characteristics of snake, which we remember from previous perceptions, on the rope. Following this general paradigm, the Advaitin explains the appearance of phenomenal reality or *māyā* in epistemological terms as the mutual superimposition of what does not belong to the Self (finitude, change) on the Self, and of that which belongs to the Self on the not-Self.[3] In other words, ignorance consists in the failure to discriminate between the phenomenal world, including the individual self, and Brahman, the eternally real, transcendental ground of existence.

Śaṅkara shows absolutely no hesitation in maintaining that

1. *Chāndogya Upaniṣad* 6.8.6., quoted in R. E. Hume, trans., *The Thirteen Principal Upaniṣads*, p. 246. (Unless otherwise stated, and with the exceptions of the *Bṛhadāraṇyaka* and *Māṇḍūkya Upaniṣads*, all translations of Upaniṣadic texts are based upon Hume's work).

2. Śaṅkara, *Brahma-sūtra Śaṅkara-Bhāṣya* (Hereafter : B.S.S.B.), Introduction, quoted in N. K. Devaraja, *An Introduction to Śaṅkara's Theory of Knowledge*, p. 198.

3. *B.S.S.B.*, Introduction.

all empirical knowledge and the means used to attain it, along with scripture and all conventional and religious categories of thought, result from the mutual superimposition of Self and not-Self and are thus of the nature of ignorance.[1] Further, the nature of the experience of the individual self (*jīva*), who is both grounded in Ātman and yet afflicted by ignorance, is characterized, according to Advaita, by the duality between the subject and its objects. Of course, this duality is only apparent, but the individual, who is ignorant of the ultimately illusory nature of his own phenomenal experience, superimposes reality on duality and then tries to find the former in the latter. The individual attempts to establish itself as eternal by identifying with its own activity, "I am this" (*aham idam*), and by appropriating the objects of its experience, "This is mine" (*mama idam*). In so doing, the individual not only becomes bound to its own activity and to the objects which it enjoys, but also creates for itself immeasurable suffering by constantly and unsuccessfully trying to locate the real and unchanging in what is of the nature of appearance and change. However, the Advaitin does not think that the search for reality is equivalent to tilting at windmills. Rather, he maintains that the individual's attempt to locate reality within the realm of phenomenal experience is equivalent to running around in circles (*saṁsāra*), that is, to being bound to the world and to suffer repeated births, deaths and rebirths in it.

By what means, then, does the search for reality proceed ? The answer to this question is found in the Advaitic analysis of error. The Advaitin claims that the moment a person realizes he has superimposed the characteristics of one thing onto another, he immediately recognizes the content of consciousness as it is rather than as it appears, and in so doing simultaneously turns away from the illusory appearance. Of course, it might take some time before the appearance is lost to consciousness altogether, e.g., a person may remember that he mistook a particular rope for a snake each time he comes in contact with the rope for months and perhaps even years afterwards. Yet the power of the superimposed content to deceive has been undermined because this

1. *Ibid.* Śaṅkara himself accepts only perception (*pratyakṣa*), inference (*anumāna*) and verbal testimony (*śabda*) as valid means of knowledge, while post-Śaṅkara Advaitins follow the Bhāṭṭa Mīmāṁsā school and accept six *pramāṇas*. Cf. Deutsch, *op. cit.*, p. 69 ff.

person no longer gives his attention to, nor does he value his original judgment of, the illusory content, i.e., he no longer believes that the rope is a snake. This process, of rejecting "an object or content of consciousness as initially appraised in the light of a new judgment or experience"[1] has been called sublation, subration, cancellation or contradiction (*bādha*) by English speaking commentators on Advaita. The process of sublation serves as the Advaitic criterion of truth. And this criterion of truth, which contains both "axiological and noetic dimensions ... is uniquely qualified, according to Advaita, to serve as a criterion for establishing ontological distinctions."[2] In other words, when an illusory appearance is recognized as such, it is taken, psychologically, as being less real than the content of consciousness replacing it. Thus, the less capable something is of being sublated, the truer it is, the more real it is, and the more highly is it to be valued. Following this logic, reality, or Brahman, is that experience or state of being which is non-sublatable and ultimately valuable.

Advaitic ethics and axiology complement the philosophical economy found in this metaphysical and epistemological position. The highest value and ultimate end of life for the Advaitin is called liberation (*mokṣa*) and consists in higher knowledge (*parā vidyā*) i.e., in the knowledge of the identity of Self with Brahman. Thus, the basis for determining good and bad depends, in this context, on the efficacy an action or thought has in directing man to higher knowledge. However, the Advaitin maintains that there are no necessary and sufficient conditions and no guaranteed ethical or religious conduct for realizing liberation. In his commentary on the first of the *Brahma Sūtras,* Śaṅkara draws a sharp distinction between action undertaken in the performance of religious duty (*dharma*) and knowledge. The fruits of religious activity are dependent upon human activity, while Brahman knowledge, Śaṅkara maintains, is an eternal and autonomous reality unto itself. This radical separation between religious conduct and Brahman knowledge is based on Advaitic metaphysics and epistemology, i.e., on the claim that all relative knowledge and worldly conduct are grounded in ignorance while Brahman,

1. Deutsch, *op. cit.*, p. 16.
2. *Ibid.*, p. 17.

eternally peaceful and all-knowing, transcends ignorance completely.

In spite of this radical distinction between Brahman and the world, and between knowledge and action, Śaṅkara maintains that man's bondage consists in the fact that he fails to discriminate between these radically different orders of being. Thus, man can cancel this misidentification or superimposition through the proper discrimination or desuperimposition (*apavāda*) of the Self from the not-Self (*jīva, māyā*). This spiritual process, which culminates in the complete sublation of the phenomenal world, is called the path of knowledge (*jñāna-yoga*). Advaitic metaphysics plays a central role in this process by providing an analysis of what is not of the Self in terms of which the aspirant can guide his discriminating activity. In addition to a preliminary fourfold discipline (*sādhana catuṣṭaya*),[1] the main practice of knowledge involves three stages : hearing (*śravaṇa*) Advaitic metaphysics; reflecting (*manana*) upon them; and constant meditation (*nididhyāsana*) upon the essential truths of these teachings, expressed in terms of the great sayings (*mahāvākya*) such as 'Thou Art That'.[2] The path culminates in a spiritual intuition of the identity of Self with Brahman, upon which intuition phenomenal experience is sublated and Brahman, the "fullness of being which is the 'content' of non-dualistic spiritual experience"[3] is realized.

Before moving on to the second part of this chapter, an introduction to the Advaitic theory of consciousness, it might be helpful to pause for a moment and reflect upon the nature of Advaitic metaphysics. It might seem as if Śaṅkara is arguing from an experience to a metaphysics which claims to be descriptive of reality. Attempts to make such a move have, in general, been treated with a great deal of suspicion in the history of Western philosophy since Kant. However, to accuse the Advaitin of being involved in such a program would miss the nature of both his experience and his metaphysics. Firstly, Śaṅkara is not, from the point of view of the *via negativa*, arguing from an experience to a description of reality. Strictly speaking, of course, he is

1. *B.S.S.B.* 1.1.1.
2. Cf. Deutsch, *op. cit.*, pp. 104-110; M. Hiriyanna, *Popular Essays in Indian Philosophy*, pp. 1-18.
3. Deutsch, *op. cit.*, p. 13.

relying upon the testimony of the Upaniṣadic sages for his treatment of absolute reality. And these seers claimed to have had a realization which was so authentic, satisfying, certain and immutable that all other experience was immediately known to be illusory, or mere appearance, in contrast. Thus there is no argument from experience to reality, for the experience is identical with reality. In this vein, these seers found that they were neither able to grasp the essence of this realization nor to communicate it to others through conventional categories of thought. Since conceptual experience and the phenomenal world were transcended completely in the realization of Brahman, the need for a metaphysical description of reality was done away with altogether. Śaṅkara makes it perfectly clear that in following these sages he has no intention of trying to deduce facts about the natural order, or phenomenal reality, from the realization of the absolute. Where the phenomenal order is concerned, knowledge derived from the senses is sufficient and cannot be refuted by any amount of conflicting scriptural testimony. Thus, when the *Muṇḍaka Upaniṣad* says that Brahman is that which, when known all else becomes known,[1] it means that "all else of value" has been realized and that "nothing else needs to be known."[2]

However, from another point of view, Śaṅkara is opposed to the attempt to deny the world from within the world, and is thus committed to presenting some form of metaphysical system which both explains phenomenal reality and points us to the absolute. And he does present such a system, of course, beginning with the essential definition of reality as existence, knowledge and bliss, and with the claim that the Self is identical with reality. Here Śaṅkara gets involved in the very type of program to which Kant was so opposed through the Advaitic equivalents of Kant's speculative or rational psychology, cosmology and theology.[3] The point to be made in this context is that while Śaṅkara's metaphysics attempts to do justice to our phenomenal experience of the world in terms of that experience, its overriding purpose, and all its characterizations of reality, are ultimately therapeutic, i.e.,

1. *Muṇḍaka Upaniṣad* 1.1.3.
2. Deutsch. *op. cit.*, p. 84.
3. Immanuel Kant, *Critique of Pure Reason* trans. by N. Kemp Smith, p. 323.

are intended ... to aid those who are searching for Brahman but have not yet realized It."[1] Thus, in the final analysis, it would not be inaccurate to say that Śaṅkara neither argues from an experience to a description of reality, nor leaves us with a monument to speculative metaphysics.

Consciousness in Advaita

What is the nature of the Advaitic theory of consciousness, and how does this theory fit into the Advaitin's philosophical system ?

Perhaps the most unique feature of the Advaitic treatment of consciousness is the radical ontological distinction posited between absolute or pure, universal consciousness (*cit, sākṣi caitanya*) and phenomenal or modified consciousness (*citta, vṛtti caitanya*). For Śaṅkara, consciousness is awareness, intelligence or knowledge that can be viewed as free or bound. While consciousness as Brahman exists eternally, is identical with reality itself and is conceived as pure knowledge, "a solid mass of knowledge only,"[2] it also persists in all phenomenal experience as well, where it is called an enjoyer (*bhoktṛ*).[3] Thus we read in the *Upaniṣads* that pure consciousness cannot be "known as an object of mediate knowledge, yet it is known as involved in every act of knowing."[4] This radical ontological discontinuity should come as no surprise at this point, since it corresponds to the previously mentioned Advaitic dichotomies between absolute and phenomenal reality, higher and lower knowledge, and the ultimate value or freedom associated with knowledge and the bondage of action.

Further, this distinction is readily assimilated into the Advaitic scheme of things and does not force the Advaitin into upholding any of the types of dualism found in other Indian or Western systems of thought. For example, in the Sāṅkhya school we find an ultimate dualism posited between soul or absolute consciousness

1. Deutsch, *op. cit.*, p. 11.

2. *Bṛhadāraṇyaka Upaniṣad* 2.4.12. (*Vijñānaghana eva*).

3. *Kaṭha Upaniṣad* 3.4. The objection can be raised at this point that the Advaitin contradicts himself by claiming that absolute consciousness is discontinuous with, yet persists in, modified consciousness. A response to this objection is offered in Chapter II, below.

4. *Kena Upaniṣad* 1.4.

(*puruṣa*) on the one hand and matter (*prakṛti*), including phenomenal consciousness, on the other. In this system phenomenal consciousness, being a reflection of the eternally isolated soul in matter, is categorized on the side of matter as opposed to soul. However, this distinction is not equivalent to the Advaitin's radical discontinuity since, for Sāṅkhya, the matter of which phenomenal consciousness is a modification is as ontologically real as pure consciousness itself. In Western thought the most common instance of dualism to be found is that which opposes mind to matter. And in the case of Descartes' metaphysical dualism, for example, there is not the slightest suggestion of an ontological distinction between mind or mental substance and the activities of mind, or the attributes of mental substance.

Thus the doctrine of the radical discontinuity between absolute and phenomenal consciousness that Śaṅkara and his followers uphold does not lead to an ultimate duality between these two orders. Instead, the higher order consciousness persists as the underlying, unifying and intelligent ground of all phenomenal states of consciousness. "Reality is consciousness"[1] and consciousness is "like a thread, that courses through and holds together a collection of pearls"[2] but which is never identical with them.

This brings us to the second distinctive feature of the Advaitic theory of consciousness, its hierarchical nature. As one might expect, this hierarchical vision of consciousness goes back to the *Upaniṣads*, wherein a number of examples of the ordering of all phenomena according to their respective degrees of purity and intelligence can be found. In the *Chāndogya Upaniṣad*, for example, Prajāpati teaches Indra that the consciousness which is identified with the waking, dream and deep sleep states of experience is in actuality Ātman, or pure consciousness itself. Indeed, concludes Prajāpati, pure consciousness continues unaffected throughout all empirical states of experience.[3] Similarly, in the *Taittirīya Upaniṣad*, the essence of the Ātman is progressively revealed in terms of degrees of intensification of consciousness beginning with the physical body and the energy of austerity

---

1. *Aitareya Upaniṣad* 3.3. (*Prajñānam Brahma*).
2. *Pañcadaśī* 1.4., p. 8.
3. *Chāndogya Upaniṣad* 8.7.1-8,12.6.

(*tapas*), moving through the vital force of life (*prāṇa*), the sense mind (*manas*) and the understanding (*vijñāna*), and culminating in bliss (*ānanda*), or the state in which there is no lack of value, no duality and no limitation.[1] But perhaps the most complete statement of the hierarchical persistence of pure consciousness in phenomenal states of experience is found in the *Māṇḍūkya Upaniṣad.* Here, the waking, dream, deep sleep states, along with the "fourth" (*turīya*) state, or freedom itself, are identified as the four quarters of the Self (Ātman) or pure consciousness. Consciousness is said to be the witness which underlies the first three states and remains unaffected as it moves through them. Further, these three states are ranked hierarchically according to the subtlety of their respective objects of experience, i.e., according to the increasing purification and intensification of consciousness each state demonstrates in its function as an enjoyer.

These hierarchical treatments of consciousness might seem like the clumsy attempts of an ancient cosmologist or perhaps of a primitive scientist to link diverse phenomena and a variety of experiences under one unifying explanatory principle. In early Greek thought, for example, Anaximines tried to account for the elements and everything that exists by explaining that the original source and principle (*archê*) of all things was air. For Anaximines, all things could be understood in terms of the rarefaction and condensation of air. However, to treat these Upaniṣadic hierarchies in this way would be to miss their essential meaning and indeed, their real value. For the meaning of these hierarchies of consciousness is that the essential, unchanging and intelligent ground of existence is the source of one's own subjective experience. In other words, one can discover the nature of existence by analysing one's own existence as manifest in experience. An Upaniṣadic seer would have been shocked to know how long it took the early Greek philosophers to actually come up with a theory of reality that included mind and subjective experience. Socrates was shocked by this fact as well, as indicated by his initial enthusiasm with, but subsequent disappointment over, the implications left undeveloped in Anaxagoras' theory that Mind (*nous*) was the principle of all things.[2]

---

1. *Taittirīya Upaniṣad* 3.2.6.
2. Plato, *Phaedo*, 97-99.

So much for the meaning of the hierarchical approach to consciousness. What about its value ? The value of this approach to consciousness was immense in the minds of these seers, as in the minds of Śaṅkara and his followers. For it was by means of these analyses of the levels of consciousness that an Advaitic student could "develop in himself... the ability to discriminate the real from the non-real"[1] and thereby go beyond conceptual knowledge about reality to the actual realization of reality and liberation itself. Professor T. M. P. Mahadevan, summarizing the treatment of this approach to reality in Bhāratītīrtha's *Pañcadaśī*, a late Advaitic commentarial text, says :

> The principle which is applied in this investigation is : what is grosser and more external and less pervasive is less real than what is subtler, and more internal and more pervasive. Applying this principle one arrives at the truth that the Self is supremely real because it is the subtlest and the inmost being which is non-dual...[2]

Thus the hierarchical treatment of consciousness is as integral to the final spiritual goal of Advaitic thought as it is to the inner workings of the philosophy of non-duality itself. In spite of the importance of this hierarchy, however, no amount of multiplication of levels of increasing subtlety within phenomenal consciousness can bridge the radical discontinuity between phenomenal and absolute consciousness, just as no amount of discriminative knowledge can bridge the discontinuity between relational and non-relational or absolute knowledge. But this is not to deny that there are stages in the path of *jñāna-yoga*, i.e., in the progressive desuperimposition of the Self and the non-Self. As Śaṅkara says :

> It is true that the Ātman which is the object of knowledge is without parts; but as people have superimposed upon it several things consisting of parts such as the body, the senses, the mind, the intellect, the objects of the senses, and the accompanying pleasure and pain, the method of realizing its real nature would be to discard one after another the parts

1. *Pañcadaśi* p. xxii.
2. *Ibid.*, p. xxii.

superimposed on it, by successive acts of attention. Thus we may have the various stages in the realization of the Ātman.[1]

Nevertheless, the continuity which exists in the process of desuperimposition does not conflict with the utter unity of the highest knowledge, on the one hand, or with the ontological discontinuity between the highest knowledge and the path of discrimination, on the other. This is because the stages in the path of knowledge which culminate in the realization of Ātman are not to be viewed as increasing levels of apprehension of Ātman. Rather, they are to be understood as stages of decreasing levels of ignorance, i.e., as diminishing degrees of obscuration of eternally self-luminous and pure consciousness. It would not be incorrect to compare the process of sublation, by which the world "returns" to or is cancelled by Brahman, to the way a shadow "returns" to the object from which it is cast when, for example, the sun moves from a position behind an object to a position directly above it. For a shadow is a negative projection, resulting from the blockage of light; the more distinctly sunlight is obstructed by an object, the more definition its shadow appears to have. Similarly, the phenomenal world is a negative projection of Brahman and the grades of clarity within phenomenal experience which emerge through the process of desuperimposition represent a decrease in the power of ignorance rather than an increase in the positive emanation of, or participation in, reality itself. Reality in itself is unalterably self-shining, self-revealing and pure consciousness.

At the final stage of this process, then, the phenomenal world completely cancels itself and the self-revealing knowledge of Brahman is realized. Traditional Advaitic commentaries try to justify this peculiar procedure by providing analogous examples of agents which destroy themselves along with something else. One such agent is the powder of the "clearing nut" (*kataka*), which precipitates itself along with other impurities suspended in a solution. Another is a prairie fire, which extinguishes itself after consuming all available prairie grass.[2]

---

1. *B.S.S.B.* 4.1.2.

2. K. Satchidananda Murty, *Revelation and Reason in Advaita Vedānta*, p. 116.

Abstracting one step further from this discussion of the Advaitic distinction between levels of consciousness, it is clear that the theory of radical ontological discontinuity serves to distinguish the Advaitic hierarchical vision of reality from all other hierarchical systems of thought. For other hierarchies rest on the quantitative ordering of certain shared or common qualities, while Śaṅkara's hierarchy is based precisely upon the claim that no common quality can be found in terms of which the different orders can be quantified or related.

Let us look, for example, at the Neoplatonic hierarchy of being. Plotinus' transcendent and ineffable One or God is in itself beyond all qualifications of thought and is in this sense similar to Śaṅkara's Brahman.[1] However, Plotinus also speaks of the One as "the principle of all things"[2] which, according to the peculiar process he calls "emanation," remains unaffected and unchanged as decreasing levels of being and intelligence, or consciousness, from *nous* to the world-soul, to individual human souls and finally to matter, proceed from it. Thus, while Plotinus' Reality, or God, is not limited by any quality, he maintains that the qualities whose gradual diminishment determine the order of his hierarchy of being nevertheless are potentially in, and emerge from, God. In this sense Plotinus treats the lower levels of his hierarchy as the manifestation of the positive qualities which are latent in his highest principle. As opposed to this, Śaṅkara's empirical reality is discussed in terms of qualities which are diametrically opposed to, or radically discontinuous with, Brahman. As Śaṅkara says, the Self and the not-Self "are so opposed in nature to each other like light and darkness that they can never be identical."[3]

Similarly, the nature of Śaṅkara's hierarchy can be distinguished from the hierarchy of monads found in Leibniz's pluralistic philosophy. For the levels of Śaṅkara's hierarchy share no common qualities, while Leibniz distinguishes his multiplicity of real and independent substances, or monads, qualitatively, i.e., in terms of the degree of perception and appetition which each possesses. According to Leibniz's principle of the identity

1. Staal, *op. cit.*, p. 180.
2. *Ibid.*, p. 186.
3. *B.S.S.B.* Introduction.

of indiscernibles, the qualitative difference between monads comprises the necessary and sufficient condition for distinguishing between substances. Clearly, this hierarchy would be unintelligible unless each monad was capable of participating to a different degree in the shared criterial qualities.

Given the radical discontinuity between absolute and modified reality in Advaitic thought, one might object that Śaṅkara's attempt to establish a hierarchical relationship between the absolute and relative levels as well as within the relative level itself is contradictory, if not absurd. However, to arrive at this conclusion would be to misunderstand the unique way in which Śaṅkara uses discontinuity itself as an hierarchical criterion. For as radical discontinuity serves to distinguish Brahman from the world, so the criterion used to distinguish the waking state from dream and the dream state from deep sleep is precisely the relative discontinuity existing between them. For example, the intentional perception of gross material objects and the confinement of experience to the conditions of space and time, both of which characterize waking experience, are absent in the dream state. Further, the duality between subject and object and the desire and consequent frustration which characterize the previous two levels of experience are no longer present in the deep sleep state. And in both these cases, the discontinuity which distinguishes one level of relative consciousness from another is analogous to the radical discontinuity which serves to distinguish modified and bound from pure and absolute consciousness. That the basic hierarchical criterion is discontinuity should come as no surprise, moreover, for Śaṅkara's criterion of reality and truth is non-sublatability, or non-contradiction. And is it not the case that the psychological correlate of contradiction is an experience of discontinuity ?

Thus it would not be inaccurate to say that dream sublates the waking state of experience and deep sleep sublates the dream state, and that through these relative discontinuities we get a suggestion or hint of the radical ontological discontinuity that distinguishes worldly experience from liberation. But the Upaniṣadic texts and the Advaitic system based upon them are complex and at times inconsistent. And while the Advaitin argues for additional criteria in terms of which to establish his hierarchy of consciousness, he also presents alternate hierarchies which, for example, treat waking experience as paradigmatic of the sublation of the content of the dream state. These issues will be discussed in greater detail in the subsequent chapters of this study.

This introduction to Advaitic philosophy and its theory of consciousness concludes with a few remarks concerning the implications of the Advaitin's hierarchical vision. It has been claimed that Śaṅkara's hierarchical approach to the distinction between practical reality and Brahman, as well as with respect to levels within practical reality, is the manifestation of a "practical and synthesizing tendency to Advaita" which has contributed much to its historical success by allowing the Advaitin to accept "all philosophical and religious views as well as ritual and social practices."[1]

However, the claim that Śaṅkara was a great synthesizer and conciliator must be qualified in light of his ruthless repudiations of other philosophical and religious positions. How can a thinker who devoted a considerable portion of his philosophical activity to criticizing his opponents be labelled a synthesizer ? The answer to this dilemma lies in the axiological correlate of Śaṅkara's distinction between phenomenal and ultimate reality. Śaṅkara does not wish to deny that the practice of Vedic ritual is the valid means for attaining heaven (*svarga*). And in this sense he can be said to incorporate the study and practice of religious duty (*dharma*) into his system. At the same time, however, Śaṅkara considers the goal of attaining heaven to be an inferior one which depends on the results of human activity,[2] which pertains exclusively to transmigratory existence and which is thus rooted in ignorance.[3] In contrast with this, Śaṅkara teaches that the ultimate goal of life is knowledge of Brahman (*Brahma-jñāna*), which neither depends on the results of human effort nor has the knowledge or practice of Vedic ritual as its necessary antecedent condition.[4] In this sense it is not incorrect to say that Śaṅkara accommodates other philosophical and religious positions, but this is not to say that he advocates them. On the contrary, both

1. Staal, *op. cit.*, p. 231.
2. *B.S.S.B.* 1.1.1.
3. *B.S.S.B.* Introduction.
4. *B.S.S.B.* 1.1.1.

the nature of knowledge and the goal of life that Śaṅkara suggests we really desire stand in direct opposition to the knowledge and spiritual activity which others advocate.

In spite of this qualification, it is clear that the "practical and synthesizing tendency of Advaita," which has manifested in the thought of contemporary Neo-Vedāntins such as Dr. Radhakrishnan, has proved somewhat irksome to many Western thinkers. Perhaps this is because we in the West live in a thoroughly pluralistic and secular intellectual milieu, where the ideal of unity of thought has collapsed in the face of the overwhelming proliferation of knowledge in many increasingly specialized fields. Yet this tendency notwithstanding, we do find evidence in our own culture for the inherent validity of a hierarchical vision, at least of consciousness, from the fact that we see acknowledged in current ordinary language, e.g., with concepts such as higher consciousness, Consciousness Three, etc., the notion that human beings are distinguishable in terms of levels of awareness, or "consciousness."

Śaṅkara's system demonstrates that he was striving to extend the quest for unity of thought both horizontally, among different branches of philosophy and practical activity (an endeavor which corresponds to the Indian fondness for representing abstract philosophical principles in terms of practical, worldly similes), and vertically, or hierarchically, with respect to ultimate reality and value. Perhaps the words of one of our contemporaries can throw this Advaitic program and, indeed, any hierarchical vision of reality in a clearer and more favorable light.

> While the nineteenth-century ideas deny or obliterate the hierarchy of levels in the universe, the notion of an hierarchical order is an indispensable instrument of understanding. Without the recognition of "levels of Being" or "Grades of Significance" we cannot make the world intelligible to ourselves nor have we the slightest possibility to define our own position, the position of man in the scheme of the universe. It is only when we can see the world as a ladder, and when we can see man's position on the ladder, that we can recognize a meaningful task for man's life on earth. Maybe it is man's task — or simply, if you like, man's happiness — to attain a higher degree of realization of his potentialities, a higher level of

being or "grade of significance" than that which comes to him "naturally" : we cannot even study this possibility except by recognizing the existence of a hierarchical structure. To the extent that we interpret the world through the great, vital ideas of the nineteenth century, we are blind to these differences of level, because we have been blinded.[1]

1. E. F. Schumacher, *Small is Beautiful*, p. 96.

CHAPTER II

AN ANALYSIS OF ABSOLUTE CONSCIOUSNESS

This chapter presents a detailed analysis of the Advaitic conception of pure, universal consciousness (*cit, sākṣi caitanya*). The discussion begins with an elucidation of the nature of absolute consciousness by focusing on the Advaitic identification of consciousness with the Self (Ātman) and with reality (Brahman), and proceeds to an analysis of the ontological and epistemological implications of this identification. The chapter concludes by reviewing the significance of the Advaitic metaphor of light for absolute consciousness and by comparing this metaphor with alternative metaphors for consciousness.

Consciousness, Self and Reality

One does not have to look very far to find support for the identification of consciousness with reality in Advaita. In fact, all Vedāntins agree that the essence of Vedic wisdom can be summarized by four great sayings (*mahāvākya*), each of which expresses the fundamental identification (*tādātmya*) of individual consciousness with pure consciousness and with reality. The four statements are : Brahman is consciousness (*prajñānam Brahma*); I am Brahman (*aham Brahmāsmi*); Thou Art That (*tat tvam asi*); and this Ātman is Brahman (*ayam Ātmā Brahma*).[1]

This identification of subjective and objective reality with each other and with pure consciousness is affirmed time and again throughout the Vedic literature. For example, we read in the *Bṛhadāraṇyaka Upaniṣad* that transcendental, infinite and limitless Brahman is "a solid mass of knowledge" (*vijñānaghana eva*), i.e., a mass of homogeneous, pure intelligence or consciousness.[2] Further, this same *Upaniṣad* identifies Brahman with Ātman, the innermost essence of all forms that transforms itself in accordance with the likeness of all forms.[3] Thus Brahman, the utterly

1. Cf. *Aitareya Upaniṣad* 3.5.3; *Bṛhadāraṇyaka Upaniṣad* 1.4.10; *Chāndogya Upaniṣad* 6.8.7 ff.; and *Bṛhadāraṇyaka Upaniṣad* 2.5.19; respectively.
2. *Bṛhadāraṇyaka Upaniṣad* 2.4.12.
3. *Ibid.*, 2.5.19.

distinctionless and transcendental reality, is identical with the immanent essence of all things. "He [Īśvara] is above everything, outside everything, beyond everything, yet also within everything."[1] In this sense the Upaniṣadic doctrine of absolute consciousness establishes at once the transcendence and immanence of consciousness with respect to the world. Moreover, while this doctrine appears too frequently in the Vedic literature for Advaitins to deny it, the theist, dualist or pluralist interpretations of reality which could logically follow from this doctrine certainly present a challenge to the consistency of the Advaitic vision of the non-duality of reality.

In order to get around this dilemma then, Advaitins try to sharpen the distinction between Ātman and Brahman while maintaining their ultimate non-difference. Advaitins thus use the term Ātman to refer to reality or consciousness immanent in the world, and the term Brahman to refer to consciousness in its purely transcendental state, which is conceived as the utter perfection of non-duality, free from the limitations (*upādhi*) of Brahman that bring about creation and dissolve in the highest realization. Establishing his preference for the purely transcendental view of consciousness, Śaṅkara makes the point, in his commentary on the second of the verses quoted above from the *Bṛhadāraṇyaka Upaniṣad*, that "Obviously, in a passage like this, the differences are mentioned only for the purpose of cancelling them."[2] Making the same point in a different context, Śaṅkara asks why the Lord came in so many forms. He answers : "[w]ere name and form not manifested, the transcendent nature of this Self as Pure Intelligence would not be known."[3] Clearly, the realization of the identity of the Self with transcendental consciousness is the highest goal of human life from the Advaitic perspective.

It might seem futile to try to engage in further inquiry into the nature of absolute consciousness at this point. For what more can be said about a reality which transcends all name and form ? Indeed, Śaṅkara says that pure consciousness "has no distinguishing mark such as name, or form, or action, or heterogeneity, or

1. *Īśa Upaniṣad* 1.3.5.
2. *B.S.S.B.* 3.2.21.
3. *Bṛhadāraṇyaka Upaniṣad Śaṅkara Bhāṣya* (Hereafter : *Bṛhad. S.B.*) 2.5.19.

species, or qualities."[1] The only way to describe the true nature of reality is "to describe It as 'Not this, not this', by eliminating all possible specifications of It that one may know of."[2] Fortunately, however, this *via negativa* does not exhaust all possible and meaningful discussion of absolute consciousness. For while consciousness transcends the duality between the knower and the objects of knowledge which characterizes cognitive activity, the essential nature of consciousness itself is self-revelation.[3] And the Advaitin argues that it is precisely because consciousness is essentially self-revealing that its nature can be directly and immediately known (but not indirectly cognized) to be the identity of existence (*satyam*), knowledge (*jñānam*) and infinity (*anantam*).[4]

To elaborate upon this revelation, we find that the Advaitic identification of absolute consciousness with existence or being (*sat*) indicates that consciousness is the ontological principle of unity in the universe. It is the permanent, immutable, unchanging and uncaused reality which is "undecaying, immortal, beyond fear, pure, homogeneous"[5] and fully in and by itself. By claiming that absolute consciousness is pure knowledge, Advaitins wish to signify both that consciousness is eternally self-luminous, i.e., aware of its own essential existence and perfection, and that it is the unmanifest (to thought), omnipotent witness of all that is apprehended.[6] Finally, by identifying consciousness with infinity, that is, with an eternally existing intelligence beyond limitation, determination and imperfection, the Advaitin upholds the ultimately self-satisfying or blissful (*ānanda*) nature of consciousness' self-revelation.

---

1. *Ibid.*, 2.3.6.
2. *Ibid.*, 2.3.6.
3. *B.S.S.B.* 2.3.7.
4. *Taittirīya Upaniṣad* 2.1. This definition was modified in later Upaniṣadic and Vedāntic thought into the more well-known existence, knowledge and bliss (*saccidānanda*). Although it may appear that this definition of consciousness runs counter to Śaṅkara's attempt to argue that no definition can adequately grasp the ontological nature of consciousness, the Advaitin responds that his definition is, ultimately, provisional. See discussion on this point in Chapter I, above.
5. *Bṛhad. S.B.* 2.4.12. Cf. *Bṛhad. S.B.* 4.4.25., *B.S.S.B.* 3.2.21., *Tait. S.B.* 2.1.
6. *B.S.S.B.* 3.2.22 ff., *Bṛhad. S.B.* 4.3.15., *Tait. S.B.* 2.1.

Clearly then, the Advaitin is claiming that the validity of the identity of reality and consciousness rests on the existential realization of this identity as communicated to us by those who have had the experience. No argument can be offered to prove the reality of this self-revealing experience itself. Rational arguments can, however, be presented to support the claim that the nature of absolute consciousness is eternal existence, self-luminosity and perfection. What are some of the arguments which Advaitins do indeed offer ?

In order to establish that the essential nature (*svarūpa*) of absolute consciousness is permanent and immutable existence, Śaṅkara argues, according to what we will call his *svabhāva* principle, that reality would not exist at all if it were not identical with its own unchanging and eternally existing, original self-cause (*svabhāva*). If reality "were to be only an effect, then in the absence of an original cause, the effects will not be what they are, and there will be nothing but the theory of void."[1] This argument is based on applying the Advaitic analysis of the nature of phenomenal causality (*satkāryavāda*) to absolute consciousness. The phenomenal analysis offers a variety of a substantialist causal model which maintains that an effect is nothing more than, and is ontologically not different from, its material cause (*upādāna kāraṇa*).[2] In other words, the Advaitic theory of causality presupposes that there is some constant and therefore essential element in any causal situation which is modified but not essentially changed in the course of the production of its various effects, e.g., a lump of clay remains essentially unchanged whether it is molded into a pot or a vase. However, while the essential nature of two phenomenal entities may be different, e.g., clay from gold, the validity of Śaṅkara's transcendental argument rests on the qualification that the cause of the totality of phenomenal reality, which remains constant throughout the creation and destruction of the universe, must neither be limited by its opposite nor confronted with duality of any kind. In this sense there can be nothing outside ultimate reality; even the non-existence of the phenomenal world is included in the existence

1. *B.S.S.B.* 2.3.7.

2. Cf. Deutsch, *op. cit.*, pp. 35-37 for discussion of Advaitic theory of causality and for the arguments by which Śaṅkara upholds this theory.

which is the essential nature of consciousness. And in taking this step, Śaṅkara has modified his *svabhāva* principle so that it applies not only to the ontological inherence of an effect in its cause, but also to the logical inherence of an attribute in its substance. Thus, Śaṅkara concludes that consciousness as eternal, transcendental existence is unchanging, uncaused and homogeneous.

A second argument offered by Advaitins for the existence of absolute consciousness is similar to Descartes' *cogito* argument. According to Śaṅkara, "[n]one can doubt its existence; for it is involved even in doubting. Fire cannot cancel its own heat; even so self-consciousness can never doubt itself."[1] It is not clear, however, that an argument of this sort establishes the existence of Descartes' substantial self, as many of his critics have pointed out. It is even less clear that it establishes the existence of a transcendental and eternally existing Self as Śaṅkara would have us believe, for the self that doubts is the phenomenal, and not the transcendental, self.

Śaṅkara's arguments for the essentially intelligent nature of consciousness are perhaps a bit more convincing, although for the most part these arguments amount to no more than the application of the same *svabhāva* principle to empirical knowledge and the various phenomenal states of consciousness. In other words, the arguments amount to the claim that knowledge and intelligent experience presuppose a transcendental intelligence or knowing principle. In possibly the earliest of these arguments, we are led through a threefold identification of internal experience, cognitive and volitional activity, and all beings in the universe with intelligence. The conclusion : "All this is guided by intelligence, is based on intelligence. The world is guided by intelligence. The basis is intelligence. Brahman is intelligence."[2] In a similar vein, we are told that the perceptual, cognitive and vital functions of all men share in the essentially intelligent nature of consciousness : "there is nothing but Intelligence at the time of the origin, continuance and dissolution of the universe."[3] And

1. *B.S.S.B.* 2.3.7., Cf. *Pañcadaśī* 3.23-4.

2. *Ait. Up.* 3.5.3. Cf. Baldev Raj Sharma, *The Concept of Ātman in the Principal Upaniṣads*, pp. 7-8 for a discussion of the debate regarding the date of this *Upaniṣad*.

3. *Bṛhad. Ś.B.* 2.4.11.

again, the analysis which distinguishes three states of experience in the *Māṇḍūkya Upaniṣad* concludes that intelligence or knowledge is the essential nature of the substance which persists through and witnesses these different conditions.[1]

Two further points are important in this context. First, Śaṅkara argues that existence and intelligence, as essences of absolute consciousness, are identical not only with consciousness but with each other : "existence is intelligence and intelligence is existence."[2] Second, knowledge as the essence of consciousness is neither a product nor an activity.

> It denotes the ontological perfection (*bhavasadhana*) (of knowing) and not the fact of being a performer of acts of knowledge. ... [for] in accordance with the terms *satyam* and *anantam*,... true reality and infinity are incompatible with the fact of being a performer of acts of knowledge."[3]

In other words, absolute consciousness is eternal self-revelation.

Finally, the Advaitins offer two basic arguments to establish that the essence of consciousness is infinity, which is to say bliss. Infinity (*anantam*) and bliss (*ānanda*) are synonymous for Advaitins because consciousness is revealed to be full (*pūrṇa*), perfect and beyond all determination and qualification, and because the realization of perfection is the source of ultimate value in the universe. "There is nothing else which could be desired in addition to the absolute unity of Brahman."[4] Thus, the two arguments for the identity of infinity and consciousness are based on the application of the *svabhāva* principle to the basis of conventional human value, i.e., pleasure, as expressed in the experiences of love and sleep. The first argument begins from the premise that all love is grounded solely in, and is for the primary sake of, one's own Self.[5] The claim is that love is extended to an object because of the happiness or pleasure which love provides for the

1. *Māṇḍūkya Upaniṣad with Gauḍapāda's Kārikā and Śaṅkara's Commentary*, Trans. by Swāmi Nikhilānanda, 1.6. (Hereafter : *Māṇḍūkya Upaniṣad* and *Māṇḍūkya Upaniṣad S.B.*).

2. *B.S.S.B.* 2.1.14.

3. *Tait. Up. S.B.* 2.1.

4. *B.S.S.B.* 2.1.14.

5. *Pañcadaśī* 12.11-20., 12.6., quoted in T. M. P. Mahadevan, *The Philosophy of Advaita*, pp. 159-60.

lover himself. Since love is based on the happiness of the living self, the "intensity of love that an object merits is dependent on its proximity to the self."[1] Ultimately, of course, all love for objects is misplaced because "[t]his Self is dearer than the son, dearer than wealth, dearer than everything else, and is innermost."[2] Thus, the argument concludes that love of objects reflects only a fragment of the infinite bliss, or transcendental pleasure, which is the essential nature of the transcendental Self.

The second argument is based on the absence of misery and pain in deep sleep, as demonstrated by the sense of calm and well-being experienced immediately upon waking.[3] From the fact that the cessation of the cognitive activity which comprises the waking and dream states of experience is accompanied by a cessation of pain and by a positive state of happiness or bliss, the Advaitin concludes that bliss must be the essence of absolute consciousness. Further, essential bliss must be identical with eternal existence and self-revealed knowledge because it is experienced in non-duality, beyond the activity of cognition.[4]

Ontology and Epistemology of Absolute Consciousness

What are the ontological and epistemological implications of the Advaitin's theory of absolute consciousness ? In the context of ontology, Śaṅkara argues against any attempt to explain the nature of consciousness, and its relation to the Self, in terms of the traditional categories of philosophical thought. With respect to the epistemology of absolute consciousness, however, Śaṅkara focuses attention on the theory of the self-luminosity of consciousness, which is his explanation of the way consciousness reveals itself. Let us discuss each of these points in greater detail.

As we have seen, Śaṅkara's consciousness is, ontologically speaking, the eternal self-revelation of existence, intelligence and bliss. However, these characteristics of the essence of consciousness are said not to limit, qualify or determine either transcendental consciousness or the Self in any way. In fact, it is

1. Mahadevan, *op. cit.*, p. 166.
2. *Bṛhadāraṇyaka Upaniṣad* 1.4.8.
3. Cf. *Chāndogya Upaniṣad* 8.4.2., for example.
4. *Bṛhad. S.B.* 3.9.28.7., p. 567.

precisely the attempt to undermine any position which does qualify the essentially unqualified, homogeneous and indeterminate nature of consciousness that motivates Śaṅkara's criticisms of alternative Indian theories of consciousness, i.e., consciousness as attribute or quality, activity or mode, as an instantaneous moment, or as a combination of material elements. Behind all these criticisms lies the Advaitic claim that the identity of absolute consciousness with the Self is presupposed by the very categorical thinking that tries to relate consciousness and Self.

Śaṅkara's opposition to the theory that consciousness is an attribute or quality of the Self is made clear in his criticisms of the Nyāya-Vaiśeṣika school. According to Vaiśeṣika ontology, all objects of experience can be classified either in terms of one of nine ultimately real substances (*dravya*) or in terms of the various properties and relations which pertain to these substances. According to this analysis, the self (*ātman*) is only one of these nine real substances. But what really distinguishes this system, and makes it a particularly important object for Śaṅkara's criticism, is its claim that knowledge, or consciousness, is properly categorized as an attribute (*guṇa*) which is altogether distinct from each individual self yet which belongs to, or inheres in, the self adventitiously. Using the dreamless sleep state as an example of a case in which the self exists without being characterized by consciousness, the Naiyāyika argues that consciousness must inhere in the self adventitiously and must be a product or combination of the self with a number of other factors which are non-functional in deep sleep, e.g., the instrument of mental attention (*manas*), the senses (*indriya*) and the body (*viṣaya*).[1] How do we know that consciousness inheres in the self rather than in any of these other contributing causes ? Two arguments are offered : first, consciousness cannot be discovered in any of the other three causes;[2] and second, consciousness cannot subsist without a locus.[3] In this sense consciousness.

1. Vātsyāyana, *Nyāya Bhāṣya* 3.2.18-41., Kaṇāda, *Vaiśeṣika Sūtra* 1.1.6. Cf. discussion in S. K. Saksena, *Nature of Consciousness in Hindu Philosophy*, pp. 50-51.

2. Jayanta Bhaṭṭa, *Nyāya Mañjari* p. 441, quoted in Saksena, *op. cit.*, p. 51.

3. Śridhara Bhaṭṭa, *Nyāya Kandalī*, p. 97. quoted in Saksena, *op. cit.*, p. 51.

as an accidental attribute of self, actually represents the limitation or qualification of the self by the three contributing causes of consciousness.

While it is clear that Śaṅkara would find most of the details of the Nyāya-Vaiśeṣika theory of consciousness unsatisfactory, we observe that the brunt of his criticism is focused on the theory of ontological inherence (*samavāya*), in terms of which Nyāya tries to explain the necessary and eternal relationship between the substantial self and its distinct attribute, consciousness. The problem facing the Nyāya pluralist is to explain how a permanent substance, e.g., the self, is related to an impermanent attribute, e.g., consciousness. Of a number of types of relationship posited in Nyāya philosophy, the one that applies between substance and attribute is the relationship of ontological inherence (*samavāya*), which is supposed to account for the production of an attribute, e.g., consciousness, as well as for its necessary, simultaneous relationship with its substance, e.g., the self. But Śaṅkara objects that this ontological relationship, on the pluralist's account, is itself a distinct entity. And because this relationship must be different from both the substance and the attribute in question, it will require an additional inherence relationship for it to inhere in both the self and consciousness. This clearly leads to an infinite regress.[1] Therefore, Śaṅkara argues, the Nyāya-Vaiśeṣika theory of inherence does not really explain how the self, which is different from consciousness, can be both its substance and one of its contributing causes. Śaṅkara concludes that the position which treats consciousness as an attribute of the substantial self is false.

It would not be unreasonable to object that Śaṅkara's criticism of the Nyāya ontological inherence relationship does not exhaust the possible ways that a substance and its attributes can be related. For example, it does not take into account the relation of logical entailment between substance and attribute which was upheld by Descartes, among others. According to Descartes, "Everything in which there resides immediately, as in a subject, or by means of which there exists anything that we perceive, i.e., any property, quality, or attribute of which we have a real idea is called a *Substance*. ..." Further along in the same paragraph, Descartes

1. *B.S.S.B.* 2.2.13.

argues that this definition of substance is justified precisely because we are certain, through the "natural light" of reason, that "a real attribute cannot be an attribute of nothing.[1]" For Descartes, then, it is logically self-evident that an attribute must be an attribute of a substance. Applying this principle to self-conscious mental activity, for example, he claims that the substance in which thought inheres is called mind. Moreover, it is clear that Śaṅkara himself is committed to just such a logical entailment between an attribute and its underlying substance in terms of his *svabhāva* principle. He differs from Descartes, however, to the extent that he limits the principle of logical entailment between substance and attribute to provisional application, i.e. its validity is restricted to the realm of conventional experience alone. Ultimately, of course, Śaṅkara does not treat absolute consciousness as an attribute of Self. Rather, he wishes both to maintain the essential identity between consciousness and Self as well as to deny the applicability of all relationships, including that of substance-attribute, to absolute consciousness.

Another possible way in which the relationship between consciousness and Self can be expressed is in terms of a theory which argues for both the identity and difference between substance and attribute at once. Just such a theory is, in fact, put forth by Rāmānuja when he argues that consciousness is both the essence (*svarūpa*) of the self as well as its quality (*guṇa*).[2] Rāmānuja is torn between his desire to say, on the one hand, that consciousness is a quality of the self which is actively intentional and always changing, and, on the other hand, to say that the self is eternally, and therefore essentially, conscious. While Rāmānuja's theory of the relationship between consciousness and the self is thus dismissed from the Advaitic perspective as contradictory, since the Advaitin assumes that a substance must either be completely identical with, or different from, its attributes, we have already indicated that Śaṅkara tries to reconcile active, intentional consciousness with the eternal and essential identity of consciousness and self by introducing a radical ontological distinction between what then become two levels of consciousness.

1. E. S. Haldane and G. T. R. Ross, trans. and ed., *The Philosophical Works of Descartes*, II. p. 53.
2. Rāmānuja, *Śrī Bhāṣya* 1.1.1.

The *locus classicus* in Indian thought of the theory that consciousness is an activity (*kriyā*) of the self is found in Pūrva Mīmāṁsā philosophy. This school developed out of the exegetical analysis of pre-Upaniṣadic Vedic literature, which was primarily concerned with the performance of ritual. Upholding the position that "action is the sole end of *śruti*,"[1] these thinkers focused their attention on the study of injunctions to action and on the results accruing from prescribed conduct. Additionally, they moved beyond the basic position that "no Vedic passage can ... be said to have any meaning unless it refers to some action or to some means or fruit of action"[2] to the conclusion that the significance and meaning in all discourse comes from prescription to action. Thus it was not unnatural that the members of this school arrived at the conclusion that activity itself was the essential nature of the entire universe.

Consistent with this vision of reality, the Mīmāṁsakas maintained that there was a plurality of active selves, each of which was eternal and permanent while nevertheless continuously undergoing various changes of form (*pariṇāma*).[3] The Mīmāṁsakas treated each of these selves as both the agent (*kartā*) and the enjoyer (*bhoktā*) of the possible modes into which they could be modified. And one of these internal modifications or modes of self was knowledge, or consciousness. While consciousness was distinguished from the self on this account, it was nevertheless treated as a real modification of the self and was thus related to the self as an action is related to the agent who performs it.[4] In this sense the Mīmāṁsakas stressed a certain intimacy between consciousness and the self that was lacking in the Nyāya-Vaiśeṣika substance-attribute model.

Clearly, this theory is completely unacceptable to Śaṅkara, for whom the radical distinction between absolute, eternal consciousness and the activity of the empirical self is parallel to the distinction between transcendental reality and the world of phenomenal illusion, and is lost on the Mīmāṁsaka account. He rejects the Mīmāṁsaka claim that the self must be active

1. Jaimini, *Mīmāṁsā Sūtra* 1.2.1.
2. *B.S.S.B.* 1.1.4.
3. Kumārila Bhaṭṭa, *Śloka-vārtika* (Chowkhamba Series), p. 707.
4. Saksena, *op. cit.*, p. 62.

since the sole purpose and validity of the revealed texts lie in their prescriptive function.

> It is not necessary ... that the soul must in its real nature be the doer of actions in order to save the utility of Vidhiśāstra [written by the Mīmāṁsist Maṇḍana Miśra]; it is sufficient even for this purpose if the soul has authorship which is superimposed on it.[1]

In other words, Śaṅkara argues that the Self only appears to act because of the superimposition of the qualities of the not-Self on it : "the attributes of enjoying are said to arise out of *avidyā* or ignorance, and have no existence during the condition of knowledge."[2] Additionally, Śaṅkara argues that absolute consciousness would be imperfect if it were active, since all activity is motivated by desire, i.e., by the feeling of incompleteness. Lastly, Śaṅkara claims that it is a contradiction to maintain both that the self is active and that it is eternal, since what is eternal is unchanging, while an activity changes the agent of which it is a modification.[3]

Finally, Śaṅkara rejects two theories which deny that there is a relationship between consciousness and the self because they deny the existence of the self. The first theory is that of the Vijñānavāda school of Buddhist thought, which according to Śaṅkara's interpretation undermines the existence of the continuous, let alone eternal, self by reducing it to a series of discrete moments of consciousness. The second theory is the view of the Materialist, Cārvāka, which reduces both the self and consciousness to matter.

The Vijñānavādin is a subjective idealist who believes that only discrete, momentary ideas (*vijñāna*) or cognitions are real, and that there is no external world. One argument offered by the Vijñānavādin against the existence of the external world maintains that because the cognition of an object always occurs simultaneously with the act of cognition, the object is identical with the cognition itself. Another of their arguments is based on the analogy of dreams and illusions, wherein experience takes place

1. *B.S.S.B.* 2.3.40.
2. *B.S.S.B.* 2.4.40.
3. *B.S.S.B.* 1.1.4.

without dependence on the external world.[1] Śaṅkara makes short shrift of these arguments by countering that common sense and conventional logic both presuppose the existence of the subject and the external world, and that true spiritual experience involves the transcendence of the empirical subject in addition to the cancellation of the objective world.[2]

Granted that the Vijñānavādin's arguments hardly seem strong enough to support such a highly implausible position, it is nevertheless clear that these philosophers are pointing to a very important phenomenological fact, i.e., to the primacy of the subject or consciousness in experience, and particularly in the meditative states cultivated by the Vijñānavādins. This vision, elaborated in the context of the Buddhist tradition and therefore having to accommodate the Buddha's marks of existence, particularly impermanence (*anitya*) and no-Self (*anātman*), resulted in the Vijñānavādin denial of the reality of mental substance or a continuous self. Instead, these thinkers posited the existence of an infinite number of individual streams or series (*saṁtāna*) of ideas.

An obvious problem arises at this point. How is it possible for a theory which admits only the reality of momentary, subjective ideas to explain the coherence of empirical experience (the possibility of correspondence between our ideas and external objects having already been denied) ? The Vijñānavādin explains that our cognitions cohere because they are caused by impressions (*vāsanā*) left behind from previous experience. Śaṅkara objects to this theory by claiming that this explanation is circular, i.e., cognitions are caused by impressions which are themselves caused by cognitions, and that it leads to an infinite regress.[3] But the Vijñānavādin replies that an infinite regress does not undermine his position since each series of cognitions, like *saṁsāra* itself, is beginningless. Śaṅkara raises a more fundamental objection, however, when he asks where this continuity of impressions resides. For he argues (by assuming the validity of the *svabhāva* principle once again) that the experiences of personal identity and memory presuppose a continuous principle of consciousness.[4] And how can any kind of continuity, whether it be

1. *B.S.S.B.* 2.2.28
2. *B.S.S.B.* 2.2.28-31.
3. *B.S.S.B.* 2.2.30.
4. *B.S.S.B.* 2.2.25., *Bṛhad. S.B.* 4.3.7.

required to explain the existence of a substratum of impressions or the experiences of personal identity and memory, be incorporated into an analysis of consciousness based on a doctrine of momentariness ?[1] This argument does seem to raise a conclusive objection against any theory which attempts to reduce the self to a series of discrete conscious moments, although it must be pointed out that Śaṅkara's criticisms of the Vijñānavāda school overlook the monistic or absolutistic interpretation of its doctrine of the storehouse of consciousness (*ālayavijñāna*), which enabled this school of Buddhist thought to have great historical and philosophical influence in China, Japan and Tibet.

While the Vijñānavādins tried to account for the existence of the self in terms of moments of consciousness, the Cārvākas, or Indian Materialists, identified the self with consciousness and maintained that it was a product of a combination of the four material elements.[2] Using the production of the intoxicating quality of liquor from non-intoxicating ingredients as an example, the Cārvākas argue that consciousness is a quality of the body which can have no existence apart from the living body itself. Where do the qualities of consciousness reside, they ask, if not in the body itself ? In this sense the Cārvākas propound a variety of epi-phenomenalism not entirely unlike the reductionism found in Hobbes and modern behaviorism.

Śaṅkara tries to combat the force of the Cārvāka's empirical claim that we never perceive consciousness, except in conjunction with bodily activity and experience, by arguing that the qualities of the self are not perceptible to others since they are as different from the perceptible qualities of the body as consciousness is different from matter.[3] In this sense Śaṅkara is claiming that it is impossible to establish perceptually that consciousness exists, since it is invalid to identify existence and knowability with, and thereby reduce them to, the contents of empirical perception alone. In addition to this point, Śaṅkara objects that the

1. *B.S.S.B.* 2.2.31.

2. *B.S.S.B.* 3.3.53. Since no original text of the Cārvāka tradition is extant, all our information about their thought is derived from the representation of their position by their critics. This fact suggests that whatever subtlety and/or intricacy might have been found in the original position has been lost.

3. *B.S.S.B.* 3.3.54.

Cārvāka is unable to explain the relationship between the material elements and their supposed product, consciousness. For if the Cārvāka tries to reduce consciousness to the faculty of perception arising from the combination of the elements, then Śaṅkara's criticism rests on the fact that it would be impossible for perception to apprehend the elements whose combination is presupposed by perception itself. On the other hand, if the Cārvāka treats consciousness as a property or quality of the combination of the elements, i.e., of a physical body, then Śaṅkara wants to know why other material objects, such as jars, do not share in the quality of intelligence. Rather, Śaṅkara argues that the self, being essentially intelligent, must be different from, and independent of, the material elements and the human body. In this sense Śaṅkara is reasserting the central theme which runs throughout his criticisms of all opposing theories of consciousness, and that is the fact that self-revealing consciousness, beyond all qualifications and determinations, is fully independent. The ontology of consciousness is thus an ontology of eternal self-autonomy. And how can any definition, using concepts which are relative and dependent upon one another, grasp that which is radically discontinuous with relativity itself ?

Having discussed Śaṅkara's central objections to attempts to define the ontological nature of consciousness and the self and to explain the relationship between them in terms of the traditional categories of Indian philosophical thought, we conclude once again that consciousness is essentially one, homogeneous and unqualified for Advaita Vedānta. Given this ontology of consciousness, it now remains to be seen how the Advaitic tradition deals with the epistemology of eternally self-revealing reality, i.e., with the question of how consciousness reveals itself. Advaitic thinkers have sought to support the ontological autonomy of self-revealing, absolute consciousness by endowing it with a parallel and unique epistemological nature, called self-luminosity (*svaprakāśatva*, *svataḥ prakāśatva*). The doctrine of the self-luminosity of consciousness, as interpreted by Advaitins, guarantees the priority of absolute consciousness, both as the ground (*adhiṣṭhāna*) and the eternal witness (*sākṣin*) of all manifestation.[1]

---

1. Saksena, *op. cit.*, pp. 102-3.

According to this doctrine, the self-revelation of consciousness consists in the fact that consciousness illumines or lights everything, including itself. The doctrine of self-luminosity thus provides the Advaitin with the means of transcending the intentional functioning of modified or empirical consciousness, involving the distinction between the knowing subject and the object known. For while empirical cognition consists in the apprehension of an object by a subject, self-luminous transcendental consciousness is neither an object nor a subject and is known solely by means of itself. In this sense, Brahman knowledge, or the self-revelation of consciousness, is completely self-caused or autonomous, and eternally known, or indubitable. In order to emphasize the autonomous and indubitable nature of absolute consciousness, Citsukha, a thirteenth century Advaitin, has defined self-luminosity as "the capaciy of being called immediately known in empirical usage while not being an object of cognition."[1] The first part of this definition indicates that the self-luminosity of absolute consciousness does not limit consciousness as a quality would. Rather, consciousness is not the locus of the absolute absence of immediacy, i.e., of an external source of awareness, and is therefore autonomous. The second part of the definition distinguishes the immediacy applicable to absolute consciousness from the immediacy characteristic of empirical perception, i.e., non-dualistic from dualistic immediacy, and therefore asserts that consciousness is never remote from, or in doubt about, its own self-awareness.[2]

The basic point behind the Advaitic doctrine of self-luminosity is that consciousness is a light which illuminates itself and everything else at once. Strictly speaking, of course, this doctrine rests on the metaphorical use of light to convey the unitary and undifferentiated intelligence which characterizes absolute consciousness or the Self. And there is a considerable amount of Upaniṣadic precedent for the Advaitic reliance upon this particular metaphorical description of consciousness. To cite just a few examples:

---

1. Citsukha, *Tattva-pradīpikā*, ed. by Pt. R. K. Sastri, p. 9.

2. Cf. V. A. Sharma, *Citsukha's Contribution to Advaita* pp. 41-55, Mahadevan, *op. cit.*, pp. 140-46.

> The Self (*ātman*), indeed, is his light ... for with the Self, indeed, as his light one sits, moves, does his work, and returns[1]

> Now, the light which shines higher than this heaven ... verily. that is the same as this light which is here within a person.[2]

> The sun shines not there, nor the moon and stars, These lightnings shine not, much less this (earthly) fire ! After Him, as he shines, doth everything shine. This whole world is illumined with His light.[3]

> Of the bright power that pervades the sky it is only a portion which, rising in the midst of the sun, becomes the two light-rays. That is the knower of unity, the Eternal Real. ... That is the immortal. That is the realm of Brahman. That is the ocean of light.[4]

Śaṅkara picks up this metaphor in the course of his exposition and defense of Advaitic philosophy. His most vocal opponents on this point were those realists, including the Naiyāyikas and the Mīmāṁsist, Kumārila Bhaṭṭa, who wished to deny the epistemologically privileged position which the doctrine of self-luminosity bestows on consciousness. However, even these thinkers were not opposed to treating consciousness as a light as long as it was made clear that consciousness as light only illumines other objects and not itself (*paraprakāśa*). Against this position then, Śaṅkara upholds the principle of self-luminous consciousness on the analogy of the sun, which illumines itself as well as everything else.

> So Brahman being the only self-luminous entity beyond the sun and moon etc., everything that exists and shines does so on account of the light of Brahman. It manifests everything but it is not manifested or perceived by any other light.[5]

And the conclusion derived from this doctrine, which the realist finds so unacceptable, is that :

---

1. *Bṛhadāraṇyaka Upaniṣad* 4.3.6. Cf. 4.4.16., *Kaushītakī Upaniṣad* 2.5.15.
2. *Chāndogya Upaniṣad* 3.13.7. Cf. 3.14.2.
3. *Kaṭha Upaniṣad* 5.15., repeated at *Muṇḍaka Upaniṣad* 2.2.9-10., *Śvetāśvatara Upaniṣad* 6.14.
4. *Maitrī Upaniṣad* 6.35.
5. *B.S.S.B.* 1.3.22.

There being nothing else but the Ātman, what should he see or know in particular, except being eternally aware of himself ? The Ātman therefore is eternally conscious of itself.[1]

However, it is apparent that even the metaphor of light for consciousness breaks down in the face of the Advaitic claim that ultimately, there is nothing other than transcendental and undifferentiated awareness of Self. This point is brought home in the context of Śaṅkara's criticisms of the Vijñānavāda theory of self-luminous consciousness, which portrayed consciousness as a lamp that lights its objects and itself at the same time. Śaṅkara objects that any self-luminous physical object, such as a lamp, or the sun, is objectified by its own light and thus becomes an object of illumination, just like all the objects illuminated by it.[2] Absolute consciousness, on the other hand, is immaterial and therefore is never perceived by the sense organs, and in particular by the eye.[3] In this sense, the "self-luminosity" of absolute consciousness is unique because the consciousness illuminated is identical with, and never an object of, intelligence, while all other entities and non-entities are objectifiable, and therefore distinct from consciousness itself.

In addition to the particular objection to the light metaphor offered by Śaṅkara, it is clear that there are other, and perhaps more serious, objections to it. However, since many Western thinkers also found in light an appropriate means to convey something significant about the nature of consciousness, we will review their treatment of this metaphor before entertaining the additional criticisms against it.

The light metaphor has long had an important and even predominant place in Western treatments of consciousness. Beginning with Plato and Aristotle, and continuing through the

---

1. *B.S.S.B.* 2.3.18.

2. *Bṛhad. S.B.* 4.3.7., pp. 619-20. It is interesting to note that Śaṅkara clarifies his objections to the light metaphor in the context of his criticisms of the Vijñānavāda school, although it is clear that Śaṅkara's sun objectifies itself just as much as the Vijñāvādin's lamp. Further, the *Upaniṣads* themselves use the lamp to portray the light metaphor, and the lamp was picked up by later Advaitins as well. Cf. discussion of the comparison of witness intelligence to the light on a dramatic stage (*Nāṭaka-dīpa*) in Staal, *op. cit.*, pp. 103-4, and Mahadevan, *op. cit.*, pp. 187-88.

3. *Bṛhad. S.B.* 4.3.6., p. 602.

Neoplatonists to Medieval Christian thinking and seventeenth century Rationalism, this metaphor has been used to focus attention on the intelligible nature of the universe as well as on the capacity of the rational mind to have knowledge of reality. Let us look at three of the earliest examples of the use of this metaphor.

Our first example is taken from Plato, who speaks in the *Republic* about the Form of the Good, which is the supreme Form of divine Reason and thus the highest possible object of knowledge for the individual soul (*psyche*) or consciousness. Plato proceeds to liken this Form of the Good, as the cause of intelligence and intelligible objects, to the sun whose light is the cause of vision and of visible things.[1] Note that the light of divine Reason, in Plato's analogy, not only accounts for the power by which the soul knows but also is the source of the existence and essence of the Forms themselves. In our second example, Aristotle uses the light metaphor to emphasize the causal, or active dimension of mind (*nous*). He says that the active intellect makes knowledge possible, just as light makes vision possible when, for example, it changes potential colors into actual colors.[2] Finally, Plotinus' transcendental One, which is beyond intellectual activity but neither unintelligent nor unconscious, is likened to the sun in the sense that both the One and the sun are said to illuminate the universe while remaining entirely undiminished in the process.[3] This particular use of the analogy between the sun and the One, which represents Plotinus' development of the analogy in Plato's *Republic*, is the closest to the Advaitic use of the light metaphor that we find in Western philosophy.

The following objections have been offered against the use of light as a metaphor for consciousness. It has been argued that a causal, productive or creative relationship is suggested between consciousness and the world by the notion that the illuminating activity of consciousness populates the world with existents just as the light and warmth of the sun nourish the emergence of life on earth. Another objection has been lodged against the fact that sunlight is indifferent in lighting whatever is before it, while consciousness is highly selective with regard to the content and

1. Plato, *Republic* vi. 502-509c.
2. Aristotle, *De Anima* 3.5.
3. Plotinus, *Enneads* : VI.9[9], ch. 9.

forms of which it is aware. Thirdly, while proponents of the light metaphor have implied a universal conscious substance which is peaceful, pure and homogeneous, others have objected that consciousness evolves and is adaptable to change. Following from the theory of universal, creative consciousness arise two further objections : to whom does this universal consciousness belong; and what role does individual experience play in the formation and functioning of consciousness ?[1]

Metaphors for Consciousness

A number of alternative metaphors have been proposed to deal with one or more of these objections. Let us review three additional metaphors for consciousness — theater, stream and storehouse — and offer the Advaitic rebuttal to each. The theater metaphor has attained a certain prominence in Western thought as a result of Hume's analysis of experience. Hume, as the British Empiricists before him, emphasized the priority of individual experience in the formation and content of fundamentally passive consciousness. In carrying basic Empiricist premises to their logical conclusion, however, Hume rejected the simple mental substance of Locke and Berkeley and offered an analysis of mind in terms of a "bundle or collection of different perceptions." Reflecting his belief that consciousness is passive and changing in response to the variety of human experience, Hume says :

> The mind is a kind of theatre, where several perceptions successively make their appearance; pass, re-pass, glide away, and mingle in an infinite variety of postures and situations. ... The comparison of the theatre must not mislead us. They are the successive perceptions only, that constitute the mind; nor have we the most distinct notion of the place, where these scenes are represented, or of the materials, of which it is compos'd.[2]

The standard objections to Hume's attempt to convey the

---

1. I am indebted to the seminar on Consciousness conducted by Professor Eliot Deutsch at the University of Hawaii during the Fall Semester, 1977, for many of the points in this discussion.

2. David Hume, *A Treatise of Human Nature*, ed. by L. A. Selby-Bigge, Bk. I, sect. VI.

nature of consciousness through his theater metaphor are : that some aspects of mind might not be reducible to Hume's discrete, simple moments; that a theory of moments is unable to account for personal identity and the existence of a primary unifying factor in experience; and that passive consciousness fails to allow for the ways in which consciousness determines our views of things. In addition to these criticisms, Śaṅkara would certainly add that the theater metaphor, portraying Hume's empirical theory of consciousness, leaves us with a very limited vision of the scope and potential of intellectual and spiritual experience. For Śaṅkara, consciousness has the radically transformative power to throw light on darkness and to unify the knower with the known. In comparison with Advaitic transcendental consciousness Hume's passive theater fails to consider, let alone explain, this revolution at all.

Consciousness has also been portrayed as a stream. The most influential theory of consciousness as stream in Western thought is the radical empiricism of William James. James was particularly opposed to the classical Empiricist model of a passive consciousness receiving simple sensations. He tried to counter this with a more active, process-oriented analysis. Trying to account for the "warmth and intimacy" with which the self greets its own past thoughts and feelings, James emphasized the continuity experienced by mind. Says he :

> Consciousness, then, does not appear to itself chopped up in bits. Such words as "chain" or "train" do not describe it fitly as it presents itself in the first instance. It is nothing jointed; it flows. A "river" or "stream" are the metaphors by which it is most naturally described.[1]

For James, the stream of consciousness was neither a substance nor an entity but a continuous, active process which was selective in dealing with objects independent of itself. Two major objections to this metaphor suggest themselves. First, the stream metaphor fails to recognize and explain the manner in which consciousness anticipates, and is altered by, the objects with respect to which it flows. Second, while continuity may be an appropriate way to try to account for the functioning of

1. William James, *The Principles of Psychology*, p. 239.

consciousness, the stream metaphor fails to convey the unity and integration at the heart of experience. In addition to these objections, the Advaitin would add that the continuity of conscious experience emphasized by the stream metaphor fails to allow for the radical discontinuity which characterizes the distinction between empirical and transcendental consciousness, and thus fails to convey the panoramic, illuminating and witnessing dimension of consciousness.

The final metaphor for consciousness with which we will be concerned is the storehouse of the Vijñānavāda Buddhist school. We have discussed the Vijñānavāda theory of the existence of a plurality of individual series or "streams" of consciousness above. However, unlike James' stream of consciousness, which orders objects independent of itself, the Vijñānavādins denied that there were any objects independent of consciousness. Thus, in order to account for the coherence of experience, the Vijñānavādins claimed that the stream of consciousness has a storehouse (*ālayavijñāna*) of past impressions (*saṁskāra*) buried within it, and that these impressions rise to the surface of consciousness in the form of an appropriate cognition at the proper moment.[1] Apart from the fact that this theory taken as a whole is a highly improbable way to account for the intelligibility and predictability of experience, the storehouse metaphor has a number of weaknesses of its own. First, a storehouse suggests a static place or spacious container wherein forms reside. But the Vijñānavādin's storehouse is both nutritive and directive with respect to its contents and would perhaps be better portrayed as an assembly line or hothouse. Second, because there is no one-to-one correspondence between the cause of a mental impression and the effects it yields, the contents stored must necessarily mingle and influence each other. But this interaction is not readily suggested by the storehouse metaphor. Finally, Śaṅkara objects that a momentary, continuously changing series cannot consistently be a substratum of impressions at the same time.[2]

In conclusion, then, Advaitins maintain that absolute consciousness is identical with the essence of subjective and objective reality and that it is pure, homogeneous, autonomous,

1. Vasubandhu, *Triṁśikā* II., IV., XVII-XIX.
2. *B.S.S.B.* 2.3.31.

self-revealing and self-validating. Further, while Advaitins have insisted that consciousness is ultimately beyond determination and qualification in terms of the categories of thought, and have criticized various attempts to classify consciousness according to conventional philosophical categories, they have nevertheless tried to indicate what consciousness is not, i.e., it is not ignorant, not unreal and not painful. Finally, in more poetic terms, Advaitins have likened consciousness to the undifferentiated light of the sun, which illuminates itself while witnessing and giving birth to all creation. And it may well be the case, after all, that the most effective way to convey a sense of transcendental consciousness is through the use of just such a metaphor.

CHAPTER III

THE HIERARCHY OF LOWER LEVELS OF CONSCIOUSNESS AND ITS DISTINGUISHING CRITERIA

This chapter begins with a discussion of both the Advaitic analysis of the lower ontological level of consciousness and the criteria in terms of which this lower level of consciousness is distinguished from absolute consciousness. The discussion then focuses on the way Advaitins have used these criteria to establish a hierarchy of experience solely within the lower level of consciousness, and concludes with an exploration of certain philosophical inconsistencies which arise as a result of this hierarchy of phenomenal experience.

Modified Consciousness

The Advaitic theory which contrasts two ontologically distinct levels of consciousness corresponds to the radical discontinuity between reality and appearance, higher and lower knowledge, and freedom and bondage which lies at the heart of Śaṅkara's non-dual vision. Just as he identifies absolute consciousness with reality and the transcendental Self, so he identifies the lower level or modified consciousness (*citta*, *vṛtti caitanya*) with the realm of apparent reality and the phenomenal self (*jīva*). And as absolute consciousness is universal and undifferentiated, modified consciousness appears to be individualized, i.e., to belong to different intelligent beings. Thus Advaitins account for the variety of mental activities and phenomenal experiences which characterize worldly existence, or bondage, in terms of modified consciousness. But just what is the nature of this modified consciousness and how is it derived from the Self ?

Advaitins have defined modified consciousness, or the matrix of individual experience, in terms of the "association" or "combination" of absolute consciousness with ignorance (*avidyā*).[1]

1. Advaitins have traditionally discussed this association in terms of two metaphors, reflection and limitation, which are treated in this chapter. There are two forms of *avidyā* implied by this explanation of modified consciousness, The first is primeval or universal ignorance (*mūlāvidyā*) which is super-

Further, they have drawn an important distinction within modified consciousness according to whether this combination is active and functional, or latent and purely potential. In the former mode, modified consciousness or the individual self is the result of the active appropriation by, or misidentification of, the Self with conditions and limitations, e.g., knowing, doing, enjoying, etc., that do not properly belong to it. In this mode, individual consciousness consists in the mutual superimposition (*adhyāsa*) of pure consciousness and ignorance, i.e., in the identification of the Self with "the upādhis [limiting adjuncts] of body, sense and mind ... on account of absence of discrimination."[1] In other words, this active mode is modified consciousness consists in the endowment of absolute consciousness with a "psychophysical organism."[2] According to the Advaitic tradition, this active association of the Self with ignorance brings about an "objective attitude" in, and "self-limitation"[3] of, absolute consciousness which in turn results in the production of the mind or "internal organ" (*antaḥkaraṇa*) that functions in all waking and dream experience.

In the latter mode, however, there exists only the potential combination of absolute consciousness with ignorance. Thus, while this mode of modified consciousness, which is characteristic of deep sleep experience alone, consists in a suspension of the superimposition that objectifies and limits the Self, it nevertheless nurtures the seeds of future mis-identification and is therefore an important dimension of the phenomenal self.

In order to come to a more complete understanding of the active mode of modified consciousness, that is, of the Advaitic philosophy of mind, it is necessary to analyze the nature of the *antaḥkaraṇa* in more detail. Advaitins account for the totality of mental functions by distinguishing four aspects of mind : sense-mind (*manas*); reason-intellect (*buddhi*); I-sense (*ahaṁkāra*);

---

imposed on the Self. This form of *avidyā* accounts for the objective world. The second is individual ignorance (*tulāvidyā*) which results from the combination of absolute consciousness with primeval ignorance. Cf. Deutsch, *op. cit.*, p. 33.

1. *B.S.S.B.* 1.3.19.
2. Mahadevan, *op. cit.*, p. 207; *Pañcadaśī* 4.1.
3. D. M. Datta, *The Six Ways of Knowing*, p. 49.

and recollection-memory (*citta*).[1] The sense-mind, as its name indicates, is the means by which the mind "assimilates and synthesizes sense impressions and thus enables the self to make contact with external objects."[2] This aspect of mind is associated with the mental condition of doubt or indecision, since it provides the knower with percepts but is incapable of discriminating among them. The decisiveness or certitude which accompanies our perception of objects is thus due to the discriminating aspect of mind, *buddhi*. It is by means of reason that we discern, judge and understand the data of experience. But through the processes of sense assimilation and reasoning, we begin to develop a point of self-reference which manifests in terms of the I-sense, i.e., in terms of self-consciousness and the pride of egotism. In this context it is important to note that Advaitins dismiss Self-consciousness, if it is defined as the attempt to know the pure Self as an object, as a "pseudo-problem."[3] They do, however, admit the validity of the more conventional type of self-consciousness in terms of the I-sense, although the analysis of this ultimately illusory dimension of experience is perhaps somewhat cursory. Finally, the fourth aspect of mind distinguished by Advaitic thinkers is recollection. In addition to accounting for the actual experience of memory, recollection also serves to explain the manner in which the effects of past experience, in the form of behavioral, perceptual and intellectual habits or tendencies (*saṁskāra*), make their influence felt in present mental activity.

As a result of this analysis, then, Advaitins conclude that mind is nothing apart from its various functions, which in turn are merely forms or modes of the modification of consciousness resulting from the association of the Self and ignorance. "Desire, resolve, doubt, faith, want of faith, steadiness, unsteadiness, shame, intelligence and fear — all these are but the mind."[4] Thus

1. This fourfold division of the *antaḥkaraṇa* is characteristic of the *Vivaraṇa* and the *Vedāntaparibhāṣā*, 1.58. Other Advaitins, including the author of the *Pañcadaśī*, have simplified this analysis by distinguishing two major functions, *manas* and *buddhi*, and by subsuming the other functions under these. Cf. Datta, *op. cit.*, 48. Śaṅkara mentions these four aspects of *antaḥkaraṇa* but lists corresponding mental conditions only for *manas* and *buddhi*. *B.S.S.B.* 2.3.32.
2. Deutsch, *op. cit.*, p. 60.
3. Saksena, *op. cit.* pp. 104-5.
4. *Bṛhadāraṇyaka Upaniṣad* 1.5.3.

the tradition unanimously refused to draw the sharp distinction between cognition, conation and appetite that has both characterized and limited much of Western thinking about the nature of mind since Plato's tripartite division of the soul.[1]

However, a debate did develop among later Advaitic thinkers over the question of whether the mind is a sense-organ (*indriya*) or not, and a brief discussion of this debate is of assistance in coming to understand the Advaitic theory of mind. Śaṅkara failed to give a decisive answer to this question and instead merely acknowledged that *Śruti* treats mind as distinct from the sense-organs while the *Smṛtis* (indirect teachings derived or "remembered" from the *Vedas*) counted the mind as one among the organs of sense.[2] But Vācaspati Miśra, founder of the Bhāmatī school, argued that mind must be a sense-organ for two reasons. First, Vācaspati claimed that we have immediate knowledge of internal states and feelings, such as pleasure (*sukha*), and that perception is the only means of obtaining such knowledge according to Advaitic epistemology. Second, he argued that there would be no means available for the mind to apprehend its own inner states unless mind itself, as an organ of sense, assumed this function.[3]

Opposing Vācaspati in this dispute were members of the Vivaraṇa school, including Dharmarāja, who argued in his *Vedāntaparibhāṣā* that Vācaspati's position is unconvincing on two counts. First, Dharmarāja claims that immediacy, and not sense-generation, stands as the true criterion of all perceptual knowledge, whether that knowledge is of internal states or of external objects. Second, Dharmarāja contends that mind needs no additional means, such as might be provided by a sense-organ, in order to apprehend its own inner states because these states are merely modes of the mind itself.[4] Note that both parties in this debate agree that mind is in immediate contact with its contents not only when it perceives its own inner modes but when it apprehends

---

1. Cf. *Republic* IV. 434D-441C for Plato's discussion of tripartite division of the soul.

2. *B.S.S.B.* 2.4.17.

3. Cf. Dharmarāja, *Vedāntaparibhāṣā*, trans. and ed. by S.S. Suryanarayana Sastri, 1.8, 13., where these points are argued by Dharmarāja's opponent.

4. *Vedāntaparibhāṣā* 1.14, 16-17.

external objects as well. This key feature of the Advaitic theory of perceptual consciousness will be treated in more detail in the next chapter. Now, however, we need to expose the basic epistemological problem underlying this debate over whether the mind is a sense-organ or not, and to do so we must distinguish between two possible meanings of the term sense-organ.[1]

The more specific of the two possible meanings is the one which implies that a sense-organ is an instrumental cause of perceptual knowledge. But to speak of mind as an instrumental cause of knowledge would be to imply that knowledge is caused, i.e., that knowledge is the product of some mental activity. To take this step would, according to the Advaitin, be to move dangerously close to a subjective idealist conception of the phenomenal world, wherein the object of knowledge is actually caused by the mind of the knowing subject. And we recall, of course, that the Advaitin is committed to a realistic epistemology which upholds the duality between subject and object at this level. Furthermore, we have already seen that Advaitins draw a sharp distinction between knowledge, which is revealed, and action, which participates in the causal process. In this context, an Advaitin would be guilty of blatant self-contradiction if he were to attribute to mental activity the role of the instrumental cause of revealed knowledge. The more general of the two meanings of sense-organ, however, implies merely that a sense-organ is an instrument of knowledge. And if we agree to use the term instrument to mean a factor or aspect,[2] then to say that the mind is a sense-organ would be to say that the mind is a necessary factor in knowledge without treating knowledge itself as a causal process. This broad and noncommittal interpretation of the function of mind in knowledge provides a basis for reconciling the debate among Advaitic thinkers on this point; mind is a factor in the destruction of ignorance but is not an actual cause of revealed knowledge itself.

Whether or not the mind is a sense-organ aside, the claim that mind is a factor in, or aspect of, knowledge allows us to make sense of Śaṅkara's "proof" of the existence of mind without invoking either the notion of causality or of production.

1. Datta, *op. cit.*, p. 55.
2. *Ibid.*, pp. 52-53.

For according to Śaṅkara, "what we find in our actual experience is that it is the presence or absence of mind which makes the difference between knowledge and ignorance."[1] He cites a passage from the *Bṛhadāraṇyaka Upaniṣad* (1.5.3.) to support his point. "When the mind is absent one does not hear or see." In other words, Śaṅkara is arguing that in addition to the Self, the senses and an object, knowledge requires the presence of attention, and since someone who is inattentive is said to be absent-minded, while someone who attends is mindful, it follows that knowledge requires mind. These remarks, however, do not really constitute a proof for the existence of mind. Instead, they amount to a statement of the "existential definition" (*viśeṣa-lakṣaṇa*) of mind as attention, or the attention-mechanism, which was accepted as the starting point for further analysis of the nature of mind by all schools of Indian thought.[2] Once again, then, the distinguishing feature of the Advaitic treatment of mind or attention consists in the fact that Advaitins refuse to treat mind as a cause which brings about the production of knowledge. Rather, mind, or the active mode of modified consciousness which occurs as a result of the association of absolute consciousness with ignorance, is a necessary factor in the revelation of phenomenal knowledge.

At this point we must ask how Advaitins account for the association or combination of the Self with ignorance, for it is by no means clear that absolute, homogeneous and unlimited consciousness can be associated with anything at all.

We find that later Advaitic thinkers have attempted to account for the emergence of phenomenal experience resulting from the association of absolute consciousness with ignorance through the use of one of two metaphors, reflection (*pratibimba*) or limitation (*avaccheda*).[3] It is clear, however, that Śaṅkara did not see any significant difference between the two. To cite just two instances in which Śaṅkara uses both metaphors in conjunction, we read :

---

1. *B.S.S.B.* 2.3.32.

2. Cf. Amalandu Bagchi, "Manas or the Mental Apparatus," *Our Heritage*, XVII, pt. II (1969), p. 37.

3. Cf. Bhāratītīrtha, *Vivaraṇa-prameya-saṅgraha* 7.2. for summary of alternative positions.

The individual soul is not directly the highest Ātman, because it is seen to be different on account of the upādhis [limiting adjuncts]; nor is it different from the Ātman, because it is the Ātman who has entered as the jīvātman in all bodies. We may call the jīva as a mere reflection of the Ātman.[1]

It is because the Ātman is pure intelligence, without any difference, transcending speech and mind, and is described negatively, that all the characteristics or the apparent differences in it are said to be due to upādhis. Just as the self-luminous sun or the moon appears as many because it is reflected in many waters, even so the unborn, intelligent Ātman appears as many after he enters into different bodies and upādhis.[2]

Characteristically, Śaṅkara's remarks show his concern to uphold non-duality by using both metaphors to point to the ultimately illusory and false nature of all distinctions, i.e., of all apparent difference. But Śaṅkara's successors felt that these metaphors could not properly be conjoined without a loss of the correct understanding of the status of modified consciousness. Thus, followers of the Vivaraṇa school claimed that the reflection of a prototype in a mirror most accurately represents the nature of the association of absolute consciousness with ignorance because this metaphor emphasizes the non-difference of the reflected image, or modified consciousness, from the prototype, or Ātman. These *pratibimbavādins* argued that the reflection of an image in a mirror requires neither an impression on, nor a transformation of, the mirror itself. Rather, the true location of the reflection is the prototype, just as the locus of the illusory self is absolute consciousness. Further, these thinkers maintained that this metaphor allowed them to attribute individual differences in the potential for intellectual discrimination and spiritual sensitivity to the degree of ignorance into which the absolute is reflected, just as the reflection of an object in water varies according to the clarity and calmness of the water.

Thinkers in the Bhāmatī school of Advaita opposed this theory of reflection and insisted that individual or modified

1. *B.S.S.B.* 2.3.50.
2. *B.S.S.B.* 3.2.18.

consciousness results from the limitation of pure consciousness by ignorance. Known as *avacchedavādins,* these philosophers argued that the metaphor of reflection fails to explain how absolute consciousness, which has no sensible qualities, can be reflected. Instead, they pointed to the stock example of a jar that appears to limit or separate the space (*ākāśa*) within it from infinite space outside and claimed that this was analogous to the nature of the association between ignorance and the absolute. On this metaphor, there is still only one Self, although it appears to be separated, just as there is one space that is assumed to be divided. However, this metaphor suggests a greater degree of empirical reality for individual consciousness than does the reflection metaphor because limitation implies that ignorance actually separates the universal Self, at least phenomenally. Further, this theory came under sharp attack from *pratibimbavādins* because it suggests that the individual self is the locus of ignorance. How, the *pratibimbavādins* asked, can modified consciousness be the ground or support for the limiting adjunct which produces it ?[1]

Moving beyond the discussion of the intricacies involved with each of these metaphors, it is clear that they both attempt to convey an essential feature of the Advaitic theory of consciousness, i.e., that modified or phenomenal consciousness is a product of, but not different from, absolute consciousness. In other words, essentially unchanging absolute consciousness is not really modified or phenomenalized through the manifestation of the individual self. Rather, non-dual reality only appears to be individualized while remaining essentially undifferentiated. Thus the radical ontological distinction between the two levels of consciousness consists precisely in the fact that the higher level is reality and truth while the lower level is appearance and falsity. That is, the distinction between the two levels means that the two levels are distinct but not different from one another. This contrast between the terms distinction and discontinuity on the one hand and difference on the other is central to the Advaitic theory of levels of consciousness. Two entities are

1. Cf. Mahadevan, *op. cit.*, pp. 218-226; Deutsch, *op. cit.*, pp. 51-54, for a more complete discussion of these positions in traditional Advaitic literature. A third position, Sureśvara's *ābhāsa-vāda,* was also suggested in this context, but as it is actually a subtle variation of the *pratibimbavāda* position it need not concern us here.

different from one another only if they are equally real, or equally apparent, but two entities are distinct when one can be sublated, cancelled or contradicted by the other. In other words, the sublation of one thing by another means that the former is both rejected and disvalued as a result of the experience of the latter. Of course, while every instance of sublation entails the experience of discontinuity, it is not the case that every experience of discontinuity points to the radical ontological distinction between modified and absolute consciousness. For, as we will see below, the Advaitin posits a hierarchy of discontinuous experience within the realm of modified consciousness as well as between modified and absolute consciousness.

Thus, the reflection and limitation metaphors indicate on the one hand that modified consciousness is never different from absolute consciousness, and on the other hand that the ontological distinction or discontinuity between the two collapses in the light of higher knowledge. In support of this point, Śaṅkara says :

> [j]ust as the knowledge of the rope destroys the serpent which appears on it through ignorance, even so, the illusory nature of the individual soul, so far as it is erroneously understood to be separate and distinct from the highest God ... vanishes the moment there arises the true knowledge.[1]

In this sense it is clear that the reflection and limitation metaphors point to the Advaitic theory of the radical ontological discontinuity between the levels of consciousness and provide the Advaitin with a means of accounting for both individuality and the unqualified identity of reality while categorically denying difference at the same time. Further, although the realization of absolute consciousness contradicts, sublates or cancels the appearance of modified consciousness, and thus amounts to the most fundamental of the criteria distinguishing the two levels, Śaṅkara suggests a number of additional criteria in terms of which this distinction can be elaborated.

For example, Śaṅkara claims that pure consciousness is autonomous and self-sufficient, but that these qualities are lacking in modified consciousness. While the Ātman is independent of

1. *B.S.S.B.* 1.3.19.

the individual, the individual depends on the Ātman, since "imagined things cannot exist apart from the support, on account of which, they are imagined."[1] Thus absolute consciousness is free and creative, and only appears to be bound and limited. Similarly, authenticity, certainty and unqualified satisfaction are criteria which distinguish the realization of pure consciousness from individual experience. Śaṅkara says that absolute consciousness is "like health, which means the absence of any signs of disease"[2] in the sense that it is completely beyond the affliction, fear and doubt[3] which accompany phenomenal experience. Finally, individuality is characterized by duality because ignorance, which reflects or limits the non-dual Self, contains the seeds of subject-object, knower-known duality within it.[4] Whether actual, as in waking and dream experience, or potential, as in deep sleep, these tendencies (*saṁskāra*) lead the individual to identify with the activities of knowing, doing and enjoying, which take place under the conditions of space, time and causality.[5] Indeed, it would not be incorrect to identify the conditions of space, time and causality with duality itself, and to use these as additional criteria for distinguishing modified from absolute consciousness.

The following criteria thus serve to distinguish the Self from phenomenal consciousness : non-sublatability (non-contradiction, non-cancellation) vs. sublatability; autonomy (purity, permanence) vs. dependence (limitation, bondage); certainty (authentic fulfillment) vs. doubt (insecurity); and non-duality (non-temporality, non-spaciality, non-causality) vs. duality. Further, in light of our previous discussion concerning the nature of distinction in Advaita, we would expect to find that these criteria are applicable not only to the radical ontological discontinuity between absolute and modified consciousness, but to other experiences of discontinuity as well. And this is precisely what we do find, for these same criteria are used by Advaitins to establish a hierarchy among the various states of phenomenal or

1. *B.S.S.B.* 1.3.19.; cf. *B.S.S.B.* 1.1.17.
2. *B.S.S.B.* 4.4.2.
3. *B.S.S.B.* 3.3.32., 1.1.4.
4. *B.S.S.B.* Introduction.
5. *B.S.S.B.* 4.1.13.

modified consciousness. The rest of this chapter and the whole of the next will be devoted to a study of the way these criteria are used to develop the Advaitic hierarchical vision. Before we get too deeply involved in this study, however, let us address two somewhat related objections which can be raised against the Advaitin's hierarchical vision of consciousness as presented up to this point.

The first objection is this. How can the Advaitin maintain that absolute consciousness persists in modified consciousness, i.e., throughout all states of individual experience, while arguing for the radical discontinuity between the two levels of consciousness at the same time ? Alternatively, this objection can be stated in these terms : if a radical ontological distinction is drawn between two levels, then how can the same predicate, e.g., consciousness, experience, truth or reality, be used to describe both ? One of the possible responses that an Advaitin might offer to these objections proceeds along the following lines. First, the claim that absolute consciousness persists through all phenomenal experience is not meant to imply that the Self really becomes, or is modified into, individual experience. Rather, the Self remains as the eternal ground of all apparent individuality, but is realized as such only upon the cancellation of appearance. In other words, modified consciousness does not become the Self. Only through the cancellation of individuality is absolute consciousness known to have "persisted" all along.

Second, Advaitins have long recognized that there is an ambiguity involved in using the same concepts to refer to two radically distinct levels. Śankara himself says that what we call modified consciousness, conventional experience, or pragmatic truth is ultimately rooted in ignorance, opposed to the full consciousness of Ātman and, in this sense, "unconscious."[1] Nevertheless, the Advaitin maintains that we are justified in calling ignorance relative consciousness, even though it is not absolute consciousness, because modified consciousness is the only kind of intelligence with which we are conventionally familiar and to which our universe of discourse refers. Ultimately, however, absolute consciousness stands beyond the grasp of language. Thus, the act of calling individuality modified consciousness is nothing more than a "courtesy" to ignorance itself.

1. *B.S.S.B.* 1.1. Introduction.

But this response leads to the second of the two objections to the Advaitic hierarchy of consciousness. On what basis does the Advaitin make this concession to ignorance ? Can the criteria used to distinguish modified from absolute consciousness be valid if they are elaborated in terms of concepts which are ultimately illusory or false ? In answer to these questions the Advaitin maintains that the hierarchical criteria he presents are indeed valid, and that this concession to ignorance is warranted when the nature of the validity of these criteria is understood. And in order to clarify the nature of this validity, we need to recall that the Advaitin draws an equally sharp distinction between illusion or falsity (*mithyā*) and unreality or non-being (*asat*) on the one hand as he draws between reality and illusion on the other. Thus, while the content of phenomenal experience is false and can be cancelled, the "content" of unreality cannot be a datum of phenomenal experience and therefore cannot be contradicted. Rather, the unreal is "self-contradictoriness."[1] In this sense, then, the validity of illusory phenomenal experience consists in the fact that it does not contradict itself, but allows for the development of coherent understanding within its own limits. Thus, the criteria used to distinguish relative experience from absolute consciousness actually represent the attempt of phenomenal consciousness to define the limits within which it functions.

But why bother to go along with this attempt on the part of ignorance to understand itself, and why allow pure consciousness to be compromised by referring to ignorance as modified consciousness ? Because, the Advaitin argues, the only understanding that is available to phenomenal consciousness in its attempt to transcend its limitations is the understanding that can be developed within the context of illusion itself. But the Advaitin's attempt to develop an understanding of the limits of phenomenal consciousness is not aimed at the accumulation of understanding, or relative knowledge. Rather, the purpose behind this endeavor is a fundamentally "negative" one, i.e. to use illusory experience to get rid of, or negate, illusion. Thus, Madhusūdana opens his *Advaitasiddhi* by remarking that the relative knowledge of the "falsity of the 'other' (world) is a propaedeutic to the

1. Deutsch. *op. cit.*, p. 24.

non-duality of Brahman."[1] From this point of view, then, the Advaitic hierarchical criteria provide the means by which to order the content of phenomenal experience according to decreasing degrees of ignorance.

Hierarchical Treatment of Modified Consciousness

Having outlined the nature of modified consciousness and the criteria in terms of which modified consciousness is distinguished from the Self, we now turn to an examination of the way these same criteria are applied to the three states of modified consciousness in order to rank them hierarchically. The most well-known and influential of the hierarchies of phenomenal experience, which moves in ascending order from waking (*viśva*) to dream (*taijasa*) to dreamless sleep (*suṣupti*), is found in, and is the sole concern of, the *Māṇḍūkya Upaniṣad.* This relatively late text, the shortest of the major Upaniṣads, represents the culmination of the hierarchical treatment of the psychological states of experience that had been initiated in the *Bṛhadāraṇyaka* and *Chāndogya Upaniṣads.*[2] In these earlier texts the spiritual initiate was encouraged to examine, introspectively, these different states of experience in order to discover the increasing purity, freedom and spiritualization of the Self thereby revealed. By the time of the composition of the *Māṇḍūkya Upaniṣad,* however, these directives for introspection had been extended to include the cosmological or macrocosmic as well as the experiential or microcosmic implications of the hierarchy, and refined to the point that Śaṅkara could claim that the *Māṇḍūkya* contained the "quintessence" of all the Upaniṣads.[3]

The text itself belongs to the *Brāhmaṇa* portion of the *Atharvaveda,* which means that it consists in speculation on a sacred word (*mantra*). And as is appropriate for this "quintessential" *Upaniṣad,* the word in question is the one used to begin every recital of the *Veda,* the most sacred Hindu word, *Aum.* Thus the text begins by stating that all that is manifest in the universe, as

1. Cf. Anil Kumar Ray Chaudhuri, *Self and Falsity in Advaita Vedānta,* p. 205.

2. Cf. Baldev Raj Sharma, *op. cit.,* pp. 1-10, for chronology of Upaniṣadic texts.

3. *Māṇḍūkya Upaniṣad Śaṅkara Bhāṣya* 1.2.

well as unmanifest reality, is represented by the symbol *Aum.*[1] Further, reality is said to have four quarters (*pāda*),[2] which are identified with the three states of modified consciousness and with the Self-realization of Ātman, or the fourth (*turīya*), respectively.[3] Finally, each of the three states is identified with the syllables A, U, and M,[4] and the 'fourth', or unmanifest, absolute consciousness, is identified with transcendental, 'soundless' (*amātra*) *Aum*, which is realized upon the sublation of the sounds of *Aum*[5] and is thus beyond the three phenomenal states of experience.[6]

According to the Advaitic interpretation of this text, then, we are being directed to meditate on the letter A in the sound *Aum* in order to become aware of the nature of the waking state of experience. And once we have become aware of its prominent and all-pervasive but illusory nature, we withdraw our attention from, or sublate, it.[7] Similarly, we repeat this process with the letters U (which is superior to A and in the middle) and M (in which all sounds become one) until we become aware of the illusory nature of dream and deep sleep and are thus able to transcend them. Concludes Śaṅkara :

> By the knowledge of these three [waking, dream and deep sleep] one after another, and consequently, by the negation of the three states the *Turīya,* non-dual, birthless and fearless, which alone is the Supreme Reality, is revealed.[8]

One might be prompted to dismiss this introspective, meditative process as utter nonsense. Since the spiritual process suggested is not the major concern of our analysis of the this text, however. we can only pause to mention the explanation of this method offered by the Neo-Vedāntin, K. C. Bhattacharyya.

---

1. *Māṇḍūkya Upaniṣad* 1.1.
2. *Ibid.*, 1.2.
3. *Ibid.*, 1.3-7.
4. *Ibid.*, 1.8.
5. *Ibid.*, 1.11., Gauḍapāda Kārikā 23 and Śaṅkara's Commentary. The point behind this remark is that one has identified the letter M with the deep sleep state, and upon cancelling this highest phenomenal state realizes the Self.
6. *Māṇḍūkya Upaniṣad* 1.12.
7. *Ibid.*, Gauḍapāda Kārikā 19, 23, and Śaṅkara's Commentary.
8. *Ibid.*, Gauḍapāda Kārikā 89, and Śaṅkara's Commentary.

> The method of attaining this ecstasy [*turīya*] is not the method of scientific investigation. A phenomenon has not only a relational aspect but also an intrinsic *aesthetic* aspect merging into a mystic aspect. The former aspect is caught by our discursive reason, the latter by imagination which is in fact intuitive reason. ... This imaginative isolation is effected by prolonged attention. Discursive thought about the relations of an object may no doubt help in this imaginative isolation. ... but with science and philosophy one quite loses sight of the other discipline, viz., that of contemplating an individual object, of getting glued down to it ... by suppressing within us the urgency of distracting desire.[1]

What is of major concern to us, however, is the basis upon which the *Māṇḍūkya Upaniṣad* orders the waking, dream and deep sleep states in terms of decreasing degrees of ignorance and bondage. Clearly, the text is claiming that waking experience is cancelled by dream, and dream experience by deep sleep. But how is this criterion being applied ?[2] One way to come to grips with this question is to isolate some aspect of experience that is lost or "discontinued" in the transition from the waking to the dream state and ask why the loss of this aspect is seen to represent a movement from the relatively less real to the relatively more real.

According to the text, waking consciousness is characterized by the awareness of, and identification with, gross (material) external objects known through the various sense organs. On the other hand, dream consciousness is characterized by the awareness of subtle internal objects and by the suspension of

1. Krishnachandra Bhattacharyya, "Studies in Vedantism," *Studies in Philosophy*, ed. by Gopinath Bhattacharyya, I., pp. 27-28.

2. Cf. Gauḍapāda Kārikā 2.7 and Śaṅkara's Commentary, where the point is made that waking experience is contradicted in dream. Of course, Gauḍapāda was labelled a "crypto-Buddhist" for just these kinds of statements, which seem to undermine the relative reality of the phenomenal world. Śaṅkara's arguments for the opposite position, i.e., that dreams are sublated by waking, are elaborated in our subsequent discussion. It is important to bear in mind that, in addition to referring to actual waking, dream and deep sleep experience, each of these lower levels also serves as a metaphor or paradigm for other dimensions of phenomenal consciousness, i.e., bondage, fantasy and wish-fulfillment, and harmony and well-being, respectively.

sense activity. In other words, while awareness of the external world is discontinued in the dream state, the whole of the individual's interior mental life is placed before him. That is, the waking individual "completely forgets itself" through its identification with external objects and with its own physical body, but this self-denial is precisely what is cancelled or discontinued with the emergence of the inner life of dream consciousness.[1] Similarly, in deep sleep there is the discontinuity not only of the awareness of external objects but of the individual's internal mental content as well. In other words, the active mode of modified consciousness is cancelled in deep sleep and an undifferentiated mass of consciousness remains. Thus, the individual's loss of itself, or "self-forgetfulness" in its own desires and mental images is cancelled and the *jīva* remains in an "immediately conscious attitude." Nevertheless, this potential mode of modified consciousness is "consciousness of a blank only,"[2] i.e., of pure *avidyā*, the latent cause of all future distinctions and actions. In this sense, the dreamless state represents only the possibility of knowledge of reality, but this is enough to establish its discontinuity from the waking and dream states and to justify its greater relative reality according to the hierarchical criterion of non-sublatability.

Similarly, the text makes clear that the waking, dream, deep sleep hierarchy is also ordered according to the criterion of autonomy, which is associated with homogeneity, purity and permanence, as opposed to dependence, limitation and bondage. The text argues that waking consciousness is not only limited to sense perception of external objects, but that it is also restricted or bound to the concerns of the gross physical body. On the other hand, dream experience is characterized as perception without sensation, which means that it is neither confined to the necessary and predictable conditions of waking experience nor to the desires associated with a body. Thus, the increased freedom of dream consciousness is demonstrated by the fact that violations of the continuity of the conditions of waking experience, e.g., space, time, causality, etc., are not met with surprise or bewilderment in the dream state.[3] The dream subject has

1. *Ibid.*, p. 29.
2. *Ibid.*, p. 26.
3. *Ibid.*, p. 12.

more control over, and detachment from, the content it experiences and is freer because it is not limited to the demands of waking life, i.e., it "is wider in *possibility* than the waking world."[1] And the increased purity or homogeneity of dream consciousness is demonstrated by the fact that while dream content is composed of impressions carried over from waking consciousness, the dreamer himself is the cause of creation of the dream.[2] In other words, dream content is more subtle and more unified than the objects of waking experience. But the dream state is not the limit of the autonomy to be found in modified consciousness, for the individual does identify with, and become bound to, the content of dream. Indeed, Śaṅkara maintains that one is not in complete control of his dream because the law of cause and effect (*karman*) is still at work : "the creation in the dream ... is for the purpose of causing joy and fear to the dreamer in accordance with his good or bad deeds."[3]

Not surprisingly, then, we find that the criterion of autonomy also serves to distinguish deep sleep from dream, for in deep sleep all content and conditions are held in abeyance. In this sense deep sleep consciousness is dissociated from sensation and perception, from the body and the mind, and is free from the limitations of both. Deep sleep consciousness is purer than dream because it is homogeneous, a unified and undifferentiated mass of consciousness. However, deep sleep is not freedom (*turīya*) itself, for in deep sleep there exists the absence of limitation and the force of ignorance but not the positive presence of non-duality, i.e., knowledge of Brahman.

Finally the *Māṇḍūkya Upaniṣad* employs the two remaining criteria, non-duality vs. duality and authenticity vs. doubt, to order the three psychological states of modified consciousness. We have already seen that dream experience is characterized by the greater freedom it affords with respect to the conditions that limit waking experience, i.e., spatiotemporal and causal relationships. Another way of making this same point is to say that the strict duality characteristic of the waking subject, who relates to spatialized objects as a temporal succession of causal events, is

1. *Ibid.*, p. 14.
2. *B.S.S.B.* 3.2.4.
3. *Ibid.*, 3.2.4.

undermined in dream experience. Further, the dream experience is more authentic or fulfilling than waking consciousness because the dream subject is able to create the fulfillment of (sub-conscious) wishes and fantasies which remain obscured and a source of frustration to waking consciousness. Applying these same two criteria to the experience of deep sleep we note that duality is altogether transcended in blissful union with the Self. Dreamless sleep is a state in which the individual "returns for a while to the deeper self in order to recover from fatigue."[1] Thus, Śaṅkara comments :

> (At the time of deep sleep) the mind is free from the miseries of the efforts made on account of the states of the mind being involved in the relationship of subject and object : therefore, it is ... endowed with an abundance of bliss.[2]

Clearly, this hierarchical treatment of the psychological states of modified consciousness consists in applying the same criteria in terms of which the Self is distinguished from the phenomenal individual to phenomenal experience. In this sense the hierarchy within modified consciousness is based on the increasing consolidation of the individual subject, i.e., on the withdrawal of the subject from phenomenal or dualistic "objectivity". In other words, the hierarchy is based on increasing degrees of interiorization or unification of modified consciousness within itself. Thus we can say that this hierarchy approaches reality through the subject, or through the unity of individual consciousness, although individuality itself never transcends either the active or potential limitations of *avidyā* and is therefore unable to attain complete identification with the Self.

We find confirmation in the *Taittirīya Upaniṣad* for our remarks concerning the hierarchy of psychological states. The *Taittirīya* presents a hierarchy consisting of five sheaths (*kośa*) which cover or obscure the Self and which correspond to the three states of modified consciousness found in the *Māṇḍūkya*. The hierarchy of sheaths moves from the grossest state of experience to the most subtle, from the most imperfect and unfulfilling

1. Sarvepalli Radhakrishnan, trans. *The Principal Upaniṣads*, p. 456 n.1.
2. *Māṇḍūkya Upaniṣad Śaṅkara Bhāṣya* 1.5.

conditions to the highest degree of relative perfection and fulfillment that individual consciousness can enjoy.[1] The lowest level of this hierarchy, then, is the sheath of food or matter (*annamaya-kośa*) which corresponds to waking consciousness and the identification of the individual with its physical or gross body (*sthūla-śarīra*). Sublating this sheath is the subtle body (*sūkṣma-śarīra*) which corresponds to the dream state of consciousness and consists of three sheaths : vitality (*prāṇamayakośa*); mind (*manomayakośa*); and understanding (*vijñānamayakośa*). Finally, the text discusses the most subtle and pure sheath, that of bliss (*ānandamayakośa*), which corresponds to deep sleep and is called the causal body (*kāraṇa-śarīra*) because in this state the individual confronts ignorance, i.e., the cause of the previous sheaths and of the limitations associated with them.

Alternative Phenomenal Hierarchies

In spite of this confirmation, however, it is apparent that the hierarchical criteria can be applied to the three states and the five sheaths differently. Śaṅkara, for example, offers four arguments in support of the *Brahma-Sūtra* which reads "The dream is only an illusion; for its nature is not completely manifest."[2] Śaṅkara's first three arguments are meant to show that the dream world lacks the slightest empirical reality precisely because the spatial, temporal and causal relations known in a dream are contradicted or sublated upon waking. His last argument for the illusory nature of dream experience rests on the claim that dream-content is self-contradictory, i.e., "one event in a dream is also cancelled by another. What appears as a chariot turns suddenly into a man, and the man again turns into a tree." Furthermore, Advaitins have long tried to illustrate the validity of sublation as a criterion of truth by pointing to the way waking experience cancels the content of a dream. Indeed, even such a staunch advocate of the greater creativity of dream consciousness as K. C. Bhattacharyya is forced to admit that, from the point of view of cognitive percepts, "dreams do not deny the truth of waking life as a whole. ... Waking, however, denies the truth of dreams."[3] We might wish to distinguish this application of

1. Cf. *Taittirīya Upaniṣad* 2.1-9; Deutsch, *op. cit.*, pp. 56, 58-61.
2. *B.S.S.B.* 3.2.3.
3. Bhattacharyya, *op. cit.*, p. 14.

the hierarchical criteria from the previous two by calling it the "objective" approach to reality. In this latter case the emphasis is not on the unification of the phenomenal subject within itself but on the correspondence of the individual's cognitive activity with empirical entities, relations and concepts, i.e., with relatively real objectivity.

If we look beyond the question of cognitive validity and the problems of knowledge which play such a central place in Advaitic thought, however, we find that many of India's Yogic philosophers have emphasized the superiority of waking over dream and dreaming over deep sleep for somewhat different reasons. From the Yogic perspective, deep sleep is a state in which the intensity of ignorance reduces the individual to a kind of death and thus to a state in which there is virtually no consciousness at all.[1] In contrast with this condition, the dream state represents the experience of "dim, vague, and foggy consciousness."[2] The mind functions in a disorderly manner with little thought and many conflicting, unstable and unreliable images. But in the waking state the restraining and controlling power of the will is brought to bear on the content of mental experience, providing the basis for logical thinking and self-conscious direction of the individual's activity.

In light of these kinds of remarks it is clear that Yogic philosophers emphasize the role of self-conscious will as the most important aspect in waking experience, over knowing and feeling, for example.[3] Thus, volition serves as the paradigm for the application of the hierarchical criteria in Yoga. Of course, the self-conscious willing of waking experience is outward willing, intended to appropriate pleasure or enjoyment (*bhoga*) for the phenomenal self. For this reason, the outward-directed functioning (*pravṛtti*) of the waking will is rooted in ignorance and is considered negative, inhibitive and "evil."[4] On the other hand, Yogic spiritual activity is inward-directed willing (*nivṛtti*) which arrests the activity of the will towards enjoyment and ultimately

1. Lekh Raj Puri, *Mysticism The Spiritual Path*, III., pp. 18-21.

2. *Ibid.*, p. 18.

3. Bhattacharyya, "Studies in Yoga Philosophy," *Studies in Philosophy*, op. cit., p. 285.

4. *Ibid.*, pp. 285-86.

results in the isolation (*kaivalyam*) of the Self from ignorance and modified consciousness. Thus, Yoga is "the free willing of freedom."[1] And if we wish to include this kind of application of the hierarchical criteria under the "objective" approach to reality, we would have to expand our previous definition of the nature of this approach so that it includes the self-conscious volitional functioning of waking experience in addition to empirical cognitive activity. The "objective" application of the hierarchical criteria, then, takes either the validity of empirical cognition or the efficacy of self-conscious will as the standard in terms of which man is directed to reality.

How are we to reconcile the conflict that the subjectively and objectively oriented hierarchies present ? Ultimately, of course, reality or absolute consciousness transcends these distinctions altogether. While this fact does not provide an explicit reconciliation of our theoretical conflict, it does suggest that Advaitins are basically interested in using the phenomenal world to cancel itself. And with this point in mind it is clear that the two types of hierarchies are complementary, that is, the objective orientation makes most sense to the practical concerns of waking experience while the subjective orientation has great theoretical importance in pointing to consciousness' transcendence of the very conditions within which phenomenal experience functions. The theoretical approach shows us where we want to go, i.e., to the interiorization and unification of consciousness, while the practical approach indicates the means to achieve that end, i.e., through Advaitic knowledge or Yogic will. The theoretical hierarchy emphasizes that realization of Brahman is our natural birthright once we can free ourselves from ignorance. The practical hierarchy emphasizes the struggle involved in actually attaining that realization through either knowledge or will. The theoretical hierarchy is offered from the internal point of view of the unified subject and expresses the innermost truth. The practical hierarchy presents what we might call the external point of view and, in elevating the waking world of appearance as the highest phenomenal level, represents the intensification of duality which, from the internal point of view, is a negative projection and a mistake. Thus, while one does not actually realize Brahman in

1. *Ibid.*, p. 305.

deep sleep, neither should the self-conscious knowledge or volition of waking experience be mistaken for the supra-self-conscious or absolute knowledge and will that is freedom for Advaita and Yoga respectively. In this sense both hierarchical treatments of modified consciousness point to transcendental consciousness by highlighting one aspect of phenomenal experience. Neither aspect, however, and thus neither hierarchy, can transcend the limitations of modified consciousness and bridge the radical discontinuity that distinguishes modified from absolute consciousness.

Having outlined the Advaitic treatment of absolute and modified consciousness, it now becomes apparent that Advaitins are attempting to present a coherent theory of consciousness that can account for all human experience, phenomenal as well as spiritual. In this sense it is one of the broadest and most comprehensive theories of consciousness to be found in any philosophical tradition, Eastern or Western. In order to begin to substantiate this claim, the following chapter examines each of the levels of consciousness according to the order presented in the *Māṇḍūyka Upaniṣad*, i.e., waking, dream, deep sleep and *turīya*, and compares these with a number of Western theories of consciousness whose insight the Advaitins both anticipate and integrate into their own system.

CHAPTER IV

ADVAITIC THEORY OF CONSCIOUSNESS IN RELATION TO ITS PARALLELS IN WESTERN THOUGHT

One way to illustrate the unique breadth and comprehensiveness of the Advaitic theory of consciousness is to show how the Advaitin's analysis of each of the hierarchical levels of experience relates to selected developments in Western philosophical thought. The present chapter will accomplish this in the following manner. First, the Advaitic conception of the nature of waking consciousness will be outlined and contrasted with Husserl's doctrine of intentional perceptual consciousness. Next, parallels between the Advaitic analysis of dream consciousness and Freudian and Jungian dream theories will be established. Third, the significance of blissful deep sleep experience for both modified and absolute consciousness will be clarified and related to corresponding Western expressions of harmony and love. Finally, we will indicate some of the implications which the Advaitic conception of liberation, as the realization of transcendental consciousness, has in relation to Western treatments of the nature of human freedom.

Waking Consciousness

As we have seen in the preceding chapter, waking consciousness consists in the mutual involvement of the subject and the object, where the subject in question is the phenomenal self and the object is either some discerned mental content or one or more of the multiplicity of gross material existents. Additionally, we have indicated that this mutual involvement actually amounts to the loss of one's individuality in the other either by indentifying with it as oneself, or by appropriating it as one's own. Such "erroneous identification" or "self-forgetfulness" can only be motivated, according to Advaitic thinkers, by the desire to find something real, permanent and unchanging in one's phenomenal experience. But this project is bound to fail because it presupposes the mutual superimposition of the real and the not-real, and is motivated by desire (*kāma*), "the only cause of [the individual's] identification with everything" and therefore the "root of transmigratory existence."[1] In spite of this rather gloomy prognosis, or perhaps as an antidote to it, Advaitins have argued that an analysis of even this level of consciousness yields a kind of non-duality, albeit a non-duality grounded in bondage and presupposing the very dualism between the knower and the known which characterizes waking experience.

In order to come to terms with this point, which may seen contradictory, it is necessary to pursue our analysis of waking consciousness in greater detail. This analysis can be carried out in terms of the Advaitic theory of perception, since Advaitins argue that the perceptual situation provides the closest approximation to the nature of absolute knowledge that the subject or knower can possibly experience at the waking level. The Advaitin's point here is that there is an immediacy, or incorrigibility, involved in the content of waking perception which provides a suggestion of, although not an equivalent to, the ultimate and indubitable immediacy which characterizes Brahman realization. In this sense the perceptual situation represents the limit of certainty and non-sublatability that can be found at the waking level of consciousness. And for this reason it would not be inaccurate to say that perception serves as the paradigm for the Advaitic understanding of the nature of waking consciousness. Now the fact that Advaitins place so much importance on the analysis of perceptual knowledge is not particularly unusual. In fact, many Western epistemologists grant to perception a prominent if not primary place both as a source of knowledge and as a means of coming to terms with the nature of consciousness. The exceptions to this generalization, of course, are those Rationalists for whom perception, although still the primary sense, is excluded from both genuine knowledge and the true nature of the soul. What does distinguish the Advaitic position, however, is its explanation of the reason for perception's pre-eminence in waking consciousness.

This point is brought out by Dharmarāja in his classic treatment of Advaitic epistemology. After defining perception (*pratyakṣa*) as direct, immediate awareness,[2] Dharmarāja goes on to say that

1. *Bṛhad. S.B.* 4.4.5.
2. *Vedāntaparibhāṣā* 1.2.

only absolute consciousness is perceptual knowledge in the strictest sense since only pure, self-luminous consciousness is eternally and immediately aware of itself without ever having to become an object for itself. However, Dharmarāja retreats from this position to some extent when he says that we are entitled to call a particular modification or psychosis (*vṛtti*) of the mind, which occurs in waking experience, "perception" because this psychosis brings about the revelation or knowledge of the non-difference between the knower (*pramātā*) and the known (*prameya*), the subject and the object or, in his own terms, between the cognizer-consciousness (*pramātṛ-caitanya*) and the content-defined consciousness (*viṣaya-caitanya*).[1] While thus admitting that waking experience consists of the common sense, naive realist dualism between the subject and the object, the Advaitic tradition nevertheless maintains that this opposition is ultimately false, since consciousness limited by the mind and consciousness limited by the object are both appearances of all-pervading consciousness (*Brahma-caitanya*) and are therefore ultimately identical. As the author of the *Advaitasiddhi* contends, "that *Brahma-caitanya* which is the unknown object of knowledge is the knowledge of the object when known."[2] In this sense, then, the pre-eminence of perception in waking consciousness consists in the fact that its immediacy is both grounded in and reveals the non-duality of Brahman or pure consciousness. In Advaita, "the purely epistemological question of perception ... is erected on a metaphysical theory of the basic identity of the subject and the object. Man knows because objects are knowable," i.e., endowed with the capacity to be known.[3]

Thus, in the context of Advaitic metaphysics, perception is the primary source of human knowledge; all the other means of knowledge except Vedic testimony, which deals with supersensible reality, depend on perception and are therefore less

1. While Western psychologists tend to use the term psychosis to indicate an abnormal state of mind, Advaitic scholars have used this term to refer to the modification or transformation of the subtle mental stuff which is prompted by the force of past *karma*.

2. Madhusūdana, *Advaitasiddhi*, as quoted by Swāmī Satprakāshānanda, *Methods of Knowledge*, p. 103.

3. P. K. Sundaram, *Advaita Epistemology*, p. 32.

immediate than perception itself.[1] But if all this is so, one might be prompted to think that in waking perception the individual attains liberation itself, i.e., the realization of the identity of the individual with objective reality. This is, of course, not the case first because the individual is motivated by the desire to become identified with a particular object and thus fails to understand the true nature of objectivity or Brahman, and second because the individual is conditioned by the impressions of past *karma* and thus fails to become aware of the essence of his own subjectivity or Ātman. In other words, the limitations (*upādhi*) of Ātman-Brahman which create the duality between the subject and the object are still in effect during the identification of the knower and the known in perceptual experience. The non-difference of waking thus fails to transcend the basic duality between the subject and object that characterizes this level of consciousness, although perception comes closer to transcending this duality than any other empirical means of knowledge.

While Advaitic thinkers agree that the non-difference between the knower and the known which characterizes the immediacy of waking perception is not equivalent to a realization of absolute non-difference, there is some disagreement among them with respect to their analysis of just what the nature of his union or identification of the subject-consciousness and the object-defined-consciousness is. Some Advaitic thinkers, including Padmapāda and Sureśvara, maintain that this identification of the subjective and objective poles of *Brahma-caitanya* is really an interconnection between the two which takes place as a result of the perceptual act. On this account, called "removal of the veil" (*āvaraṇa-bhaṅga*), the temporary ignorance (*tulāvidyā*) or non-conscious covering that conceals phenomenal objects is contacted and lifted by the perceptual psychosis of mind, allowing the object-defined intelligence to manifest itself.[2] A second theory explains this identification between the subject and object in terms of the "tinging of the subject-consciousness" (*ciduparāga*) which occurs as the psychosis of the mind contacts and reflects the object to the knower. Finally, Dharmarāja argues that the

1. Satprakāshānanda, *op. cit.*, p. 37.

2. Cf. discussion in Sundaram, *op.*, *cit.*, pp. 15-16; Satprakāshānanda, *op. cit.*, pp. 96-99, 104-5.

identification which results from the perceptual act is the coincidence of, rather than merely the interconnecting contact between, the subject and object. In this sense Dharmarāja's theory is the strongest of the three statements concerning the nature of the non-difference of the knower and the known in perception. He maintains that perception "manifests the oneness" (*abhedābhivyakti*) of absolute consciousness underlying both subject and object by uniting the knower with, and thereby revealing, the known.[1]

In spite of this disagreement regarding the nature of the immediate non-difference between the subject and object that occurs in waking perception, one common and extremely important feature of the Advaitic theory of perceptual consciousness emerges from each of these explanations, and that is that the perceptual subject contacts something that appears to be external to itself. This contact occurs, according to Vedāntins, as the mind first goes out (*prāpya-kārī*) to the object through the senses and then takes on the form of the contacted object. In this sense, then, perceptual consciousness at the waking level of experience is, for the Advaitin, an intentional activity which goes out to, and assimilates the form of, the intended object.

Advaitins have traditionally offered a number of similes in order to convey a sense of the way the mind contacts and assumes the form of its objects in the perceptual act. Perhaps the most well-known of these is the one drawn from the activity of irrigating a field.

> Just as the water of the tank, going out through a hole, and entering fields through channels comes to have a quadrangular or other figure, similarly, the internal organ too, which is of the nature of light, going out through the senses of sight, etc., and reaching the locality of contents like pot is modified in the form of content like pot.[2]

Another maintains that "Just as the molten metal which is poured into a crucible puts on the shape of the latter, the mind

1. *Vedāntaparibhāsā* 1.43.44. Although we have emphasized that these theories are opposed in offering different accounts of the identification of subject and object in perception, they can be interpreted as referring to three interrelated stages of one perceptual process as well. Thus, the veil is removed, contact is made, and the object is revealed.

2. *Ibid.*, 1.18.

which pervades an object assumes the form of that object."[1] And a third argues that "even as the light of the sun takes on the shape of the object which it illumines, the intellect which enlightens everything assumes the form of the object which it reveals."[2]

From these and other similes it is clear that the mind or knowing subject goes out through its own psychosis, which is referred to as the means of knowledge (*pramāṇa*), to the object. Further, both the psychosis of mind and the sense organs through which the psychosis extends out to objects are composed of the same subtle physical stuff as the mind itself. Thus, the mind, which is limited by ignorance and is not fully conscious, can only "reflect" the light of absolute consciousness. Similarly, the modifications of the mind, and the sense organs through which these modifications extend out to external objects, operate by serving as the medium of reflection of pure consciousness. In visual perception, then, Brahman intelligence reflected in mind is extended out along the medium of the organ of vision, which Advaitins claim is of the nature of light (*tejas*). And in auditory perception this same intelligence is carried outward through the organ of hearing, which is of the nature of ether (*ākāśā*). In each of these cases the subtle matter which comprises the sense organs is stirred up, or activated, by the externally directed psychosis or modification of the material, mental stuff which finally contacts an object, assumes its form, and reveals it as known.[3]

It is clear that this particular theory of intentional perceptual consciousness, which claims that the mind reaches out and assumes the form of external objects, stands in direct conflict with the varieties of the representational and causal theories of perception, and of indirect realism and subjectivism, that follow in Modern Western thought from the Cartesian

1. *Pañcadaśī* 4.28.

2. *Pañcadaśī* 4.29.

3. Some Advaitins, including Dharmarāja, have wished to qualify this theory by maintaining that while all external perceptions involve direct contact with external objects, the mind actually goes out to the location of the object only in visual and auditory perception, but remains situated within the body in the remaining three instances of waking perception. Cf. *Vedāntaparibhāṣā* 1.122-24.

opposition between non-spatial mind and extended matter. For in these latter cases it would be absurd to assume that the mind is in motion and that it can actively extend out into space. On what grounds does the Advaitin defend his theory of the direct, external extension of the mind to objects ? One argument rests on the assumption that attention, and therefore mind (*antaḥkaraṇa*), is not only essential to sense perception but is actually prior to it. For example, in sound sleep and instances of total absorption, perception need not follow stimulation of the sense organs. For this reason the Advaitin concludes that the senses only function as such when "the mind takes the lead" in establishing contact with the external world.[1] Another point of defense rests on the claim that both common sense and our conventional language usage indicate that our mental attention is directed to objects themselves rather than to the physiological changes produced by them within us. Finally, the Advaitin argues that the theory that the mind goes out to objects is the most efficient way to account for both perception at a distance and the process by which we come to experience a three-dimensional external world.

But this is not to say that this theory, while attempting to avoid some of the problems resulting from positing a passive subject and a causal theory of perception, is without difficulties of its own. For one thing, the Advaitin's argument that the mind must go out to external objects, because only the mind and its psychoses can reflect pure consciousness, is open to objection. The Viśiṣṭādvaitin Rāmānuja, for one, seems inclined to argue that consciousness can illumine all objects in the external world just as easily as it lights the individual subject.[2] And if one were to go along with Rāmānuja's position, then an important reason

1. Cf. Datta, *op. cit.*, pp. 61-65; Satprakāshānanda, *op. cit.*, pp. 53-54; Sundaram, *op. cit.*, pp. 27-30. It is interesting to note that at least one contemporary commentator on Advaitic epistemology has argued that the going out of the *antaḥkaraṇa* to the object is found neither in the works of Śaṅkara or Padmapāda, has little metaphysical significance, and could be eliminated from the Advaitic theory of perception without great loss. Cf. Devarāja, *op. cit.*, p. 100. The willingness to modify this aspect of the Advaitic theory of perception, which seems to be rather central, might reflect the attempt of some contemporary Vedāntins to bring their theories in line with recent scientific developments concerning perception.

2. *Śrībhāṣya* 1.1.1.

for denying that "unconscious" physical objects can actively present themselves to the subject would be undermined. For another thing, it has been objected that even the Advaitic theory cannot escape some of the factors which prompt epistemologists to think in terms of indirect contact with objects and a causal theory of perception.[1] That is, while the mind may be able to go out through its psychosis and assume the form of the external object, it is nevertheless necessary to find some way of guaranteeing the direct connection between the psychosis of the mind "out there" and the knowledge revealed to the cognizer-consciousness which is limited by, and indeed is defined in terms of, a physical body "here". In other words, one can never be certain that revealed knowledge, which is neither physical nor an activity, is in fact identical with the physical psychosis of mind that manifests the object, unless one decides to believe, with the Advaitin, that objects are knowable. Similarly, some especially strong objections have been raised in the name of science against a direct theory of perception, e.g., that the sun "sets" seven minutes before we stop seeing it, and that we continue to see distinct stars long after they have burnt out. These points stand in direct opposition to the Advaitic claim that the subject and object are identified, and in direct contact with each other, in intentional perception.[2] How can the Advaitain maintain that the mind goes out to objects, and that this activity explains our knowledge of objects at a distance, if at least some of these objects, according to scientific analysis, no longer exist when perceived by the mind ? Taking some of these and other objections against the active and direct contact of the mind with objects into consideration, Professor Datta has suggested that the Advaitic theory nevertheless merits study since "[d]ifficulties are at least equally balanced on both sides."[3]

So much for the Advaitin's claim that the mind is active and in direct contact with external objects during intentional waking perception. We now turn our attention to the second aspect of the Advaitic theory of intentionality, i.e., that the mind, having made contact with an external object, assumes or takes on the

1. Sundaram, *op. cit.*, pp. 31-32.
2. Cf. discussion of this point in *Vedāntaparibhāṣā* pp. 187-189.
3. Datta, *op. cit.*, p. 43.

form of that object. One of the striking aspects of this theory involves the claim that the mind grasps an object as a whole in one continuous process rather than having to construct the object from a series of discrete stimuli. This claim has led a number of recent commentators to suggest that at least an initial correlation exists between this theory and the notion of a "stimulus whole" or "physical gestalt" as found in the Gestalt school of psychology.[1] Beyond this initial point of similarity, however, it is clear that there are major differences between the two schools. One of the most obvious of these differences lies in the fact that the Gestaltists maintain that the structure of the psychophysical process in the brain is isomorphic with, but remains distinct from, its correlative physical gestalt, while Advaitins argue that the mind actually reaches out and assumes the form of the external object directly. The Advaitins support their claim, as we have seen, by refusing to draw a sharp distinction between the nature of mind, or "psyche", and material objects. Thus, they can argue that the modified mental material literally pervades the object and assumes its form, i.e. modifies itself according to the structure it contacts.

However, it would seem that the Advaitin's attempt to claim that the mind assumes the form of the object in one continuous act needs at least some qualification since, according to his own analysis, mental modifications go out through the different sense organs, and each sense organ has the power to reveal the property of a different element, e.g., vision reveals the color of light, hearing reveals the sound of ether, etc.[2] Thus, when a person simultaneously sees and hears someone playing a musical instrument, for example, the mind actually contacts and assumes the form of two objects or parts of the same object at once, rather than assuming the unitary form of the object as a whole. For this reason some synthesis of these various modifications of the mind must be brought about, although the Advaitic theory of intentional perception fails to take this problem into consideration and to explain how this synthesis might take place. In light of this shortcoming it would seem that the elaborate

1. Cf. *ibid.*, pp. 66-67; Deutsch, *op. cit.*, p. 91.

2. Cf. discussion of relation between elements and sense organs in Satprakāshānanda, *op. cit.*, pp. 50-51.

analysis undertaken by Gestalt psychologists to explain the mind's ability to synthesize form in terms of the isomorphism between physical and mental processes is, whether one is satisfied with it or not, at least an acknowledgement of, and response to, a complex problem.

Having discussed the details of the Advaitic theory of intentional perception, in terms of which waking consciousness is involved in the world of objects or "names and forms," it is necessary to emphasize once again that this involvement brings with it the bondage of the waking subject. This fact points to certain complexities that underlie the Advaitin's theory of intentional waking consciousness. For example, Advaitins argue that intentional perception is not a spontaneous and unconditioned movement, but a highly selective activity instead. This selectivity is based on two factors : first, that intentionality is motivated by the desire to appropriate certain objects, which means that those objects that are not desired for themselves, and do not inhibit the appropriation of other desired objects, can be ignored; and second, that the individual is conditioned or habituated by present perceptions to remember and intend similar forms in the future.[1] Thus, waking consciousness is not only bound and frustrated by its present desire to attach itself to objects, but is also conditioned to function according to the same pattern in the future. In this sense, then, we can say that intentional consciousness serves as the paradigm for the inauthenticity, lack of autonomy and duality (temporality, spatiality and causality) which characterize waking experience for the Advaitic tradition.

Some of the strengths and weaknesses of this Advaitic doctrine can be brought out by comparing it with the theory of intentional consciousness elaborated by the twentieth century German philosopher, Edmund Husserl. Perception stands in Husserl's thought as the paradigm for intentionality, which in turn is said to be the essential nature of consciousness. Husserl's claim that all consciousness is intentional is thus in opposition to the Advaitic position, wherein intentional perception is the paradigm for only one of four levels of consciousness and does not even exhaust the nature of conscious experience at that level.

Husserl's notion of the intentionality of consciousness refers

1. Deutsch, *op. cit.*, pp. 90-91.

to the presentational and objectivating function of consciousness, i.e., to the relation which acts of consciousness bear to an object.[1] What Husserl wants to define, in terms of each type of conscious act, is the precise "object" or "noema" which consciousness intends. Thus, for perception, the object or noema to which each act of consciousness or noesis corresponds is defined as a physical thing perceived from a given standpoint (*Abschattungsweise*), rather than the physical thing *simpliciter*. Other types of intentional acts, e.g., memory, imagination, are held by Husserl to have different noemata, even though the objective referent of each act may, ultimately, be the same physical thing. That is, noemata of the same object as perceived, remembered or imagined, will differ. In this sense the object of Husserl's intentional act of consciousness is an ideal unit which is neither dependent upon the existence of the real object to which it refers nor shares any of the properties of that real object. In fact, since Husserl's doctrine of intentionality maintains that the real object is transcendent to consciousness, it is clear that the sense, significance or meaning which comprises our knowledge of the objective world is given only in terms of the multiplicity of standpoints, or ideal noemata, intended in a series of perceptual acts.[2] Thus, as given in a series of perceptual acts, these noemata are synthesized by, or constituted for, consciousness into identical and identifiable ideal units, called noematic nucleii. These nucleii are free from spatial and temporal determinations as well as causal relations and thus comprise a realm of unreal entities called sense (*Sinn*), which the subject in what Husserl calls the natural or pre-reflective attitude incorrectly believes to be the real, existing world.

It is immediately obvious, then, that we find in Husserl's theory of intentionality the attempt to provide a description of the constructive, synthetic or constitutive function of consciousness that results in the presentation of an object to a subject in perceptual activity. We have already pointed out that the Advaitic description of intentionality does not deal with this function and,

1. Aron Gurwitsch, *The Field of Consciousness*, p. 266; Aron Gurwitsch, "On the Intentionality of Consciousness" in Joseph J. Kockelmans, ed. *Phenomenology*, p. 118.

2. Cf. Gurwitsch, *Field*, pp. 174-181.

indeed, seems inadequate, even on its own terms, without this treatment. It is also clear, however, that while the lack of such a sophisticated analysis of the intentional perceptual process is an error of omission in the Advaitic theory of consciousness, such an omission can be interpreted as rendering the entire theory inadequate only by ignoring the different goals to which the Husserlian and Advaitic philosophical analyses are supposed to lead. That is, while the Advaitin wishes to use philosophical analysis to discriminate or de-superimpose the real from the unreal and thereby to cancel the latter, Husserl sees the end of philosophy as the attainment of certain, indubitable knowledge of the existing world.[1] But as the existing world for Husserl is the world as constituted in consciousness, i.e., the totality of objects for a subject, the "presuppositionless" knowledge which he calls freedom is nothing more nor less than the full understanding of intentional consciousness itself. Thus, the goal of the "intentional constitution" or the phenomenological method as a whole is to render "knowledge completely immanent and hence capable of complete unification, and completely necessary for subjectivity as such, which gives it its universal objective validity."[2]

Given this fact, then, it is hardly surprising that the description and analysis of intentional consciousness should play such a prominent role in Husserl's thought. Indeed, Husserl himself has acknowledged that the "all-embracing problem of phenomenology" is the intentionality of consciousness.[3] In contrast with this, the Advaitin does not treat intentionality with anything like the degree of thoroughness found in Husserl's thought because the knowledge which is of primary concern to the former is attained by transcending phenomenal experience and the duality between subjectivity and objectivity altogether and by realizing the absolute consciousness which both subject and object presuppose as their ground. It would thus seem that a complete comparative evaluation of the Advaitic and Husserlian theories of consciousness would necessitate a study and evaluation of their respective philosophical or "spiritual" ideals as well, since

1. Quentin Lauer, *Phenomenology : Its Genesis and Prospect*, p. 81.
2. *Ibid.*, p. 62.
3. Edmund Husserl, *Ideen I*, p. 357, quoted by Lauer, *op. cit.*, p. 158.

in both cases the analysis of consciousness is intimately connected with those ideals. Such an evaluation is, of course, beyond the scope of our present discussion, the purpose of which is to amplify Advaitic intentionality by comparing it with Husserl's theory of intentional consciousness. We have made the effort to clarify this point of comparative philosophy, however, because the same lack of detail will emerge as an issue in our subsequent discussion as well, e.g., in our comparison of the Advaitic dream state with Freudian and Jungian analyses of dream experience.

Returning to the topic at hand, it is clear that Husserl's doctrine of intentionality fits coherently into the Western philosophical tradition from which it emerges. For one thing, Husserl's desire to attain absolutely certain knowledge about being through his philosophical method represents an ideal that goes back at least as far as Plato and serves as a unifying thread underlying much of Western thought up to the present. For another, Husserl is quite vocal about his indebtedness to Descartes, although he says that he is obliged as a result of his "radical development of Cartesian motifs — to reject nearly all the well-known doctrinal content of the Cartesian philosophy.'[1]" Specifically, Husserl embraces the certainty and epistemologically privileged status that accompany Descartes' "discovery" of the *ego cogito* while transforming it from the evidence for a substantial ego to the evidence for a transcendental ego or conscious being whose nature it is to be a subject.[2]

One of the regrettable consequences of Descartes' epistemologically privileged mental substance, however, was that it seemed to be in danger of irrevocably separating the subject from the object and thereby leaving the *ego* certain of nothing beyond itself. Husserl's solution to this Cartesian problem of solipsism consists in maintaining that instead of one certain *ego cogito*, the conscious subject is potentially aware of an indefinite number of certain theses or noemata "provided these theses are taken precisely as they manifest themselves immediately and intuitively in an indubitably certain cogitation."[3] Thus, part of the

1. Edmund Husserl, *Cartesian Meditations*, p. 1.
2. *Ibid.*, pp. 18-21.
3. Joseph J. Kockelmans, "Intentional and Constitutive Analyses" in Kockelmans, *op. cit.*, p. 138. Cf. Husserl, *Cartesian Meditations*, p. 14.

phenomenologist's task is to eliminate or bracket out concern for the existence of the contents of consciousness and then to penetrate, via reduction, to the essence of subjectivity.[1]

Lest this seem to be an inadequate response to the problem of Cartesian solipsism, let us indicate a third central influence on Husserl's thinking. Following Kant, Husserl limits his notions of both knowledge and existence to the realm of phenomenal experience, which for Husserl consists in the data of consciousness. Thus, he can identify the objects constituted in consciousness, i.e., the totality of objects for a subject, with being or the world. Aside from the fact that Husserl's transformation of Kant leaves the existence of the transcendental subject or intentional consciousness in the curious position of having to be "at one and the same time *constitutive* and *constituted*,"[2] it is hard to see how this theory represents an antidote to the doubts of the solipsist. Indeed, in this context Sartre argues that Husserl's conception of intentional consciousness endowed with a transcendental subject only succeeds in making it seem necessary that existence is constituted in consciousness, which in turn only prolongs the problem of solipsism.[3]

Thus, the most substantial difference between the Advaitic and Husserlian theories of intentionality consists in the fact that Advaitins use the notion of intentionality to account for the direct contact between the waking subject and external objects while Husserl uses the same notion to deny that any such direct contact occurs. And if the Advaitic description of intentionality is too simple, it can be argued that Husserl's description is both in danger of being trapped in subjectivism and too remote from the immediacy of ordinary sense experience. Furthermore, it can be objected that Husserl's description of intentionality substitutes a reduction of experience to the realm of ideal logical entities or noemata as opposed to the reduction of logical to psychological laws which characterized the "psychologism" to which he was so opposed.[4] In this vein it has been argued that phenomenology :

1. Lauer, *op. cit.*, pp. 49-50.
2. *Ibid.*, p. 151.
3. Jean-Paul Sartre, *The Transcendence of the Ego*, pp. 103-104.
4. Cf. Herbert Spiegelberg, *The Phenomenological Movement* Vol. 1, p. 49; Gurwitsch in Kockelmans, *op. cit.*, pp. 125-26.

does not recognize any other philosophical problems except that those concerning meaning and signification. All philosophical problems must, consequently, be formulated or reformulated in terms of sense and meaning.[1]

In fact, it must remain somewhat of a puzzle, if not an outright "betrayal ... of what was most fruitful in the phenomenologist's emphasis upon the intentionality of consciousness"[2] that the objects of Husserl's consciousness are ideal, and that he refuses to attribute existence to objects not constituted in a subject. Part of this opposition to Husserl's interpretation of intentionality stems from the way he modifies the understanding of the concept as it was held by his teacher, Franz Brentano. The latter had adopted the notion of intentionality from Medieval scholasticism and reworked the concept so that it could be used to distinguish psychological or psychical from physical phenomena.[3] For Brentano the decisive and indispensable characteristic of psychical phenomena is their "reference to an object." Further, objects are divided according to whether they are outside (primary) or identical with (secondary) the conscious act; unconscious psychical phenomena, i.e., consciousness without an objective referent, are dismissed as self-contradictory. Thus, Brentano's formulation of intentional consciousness is opposed to the Advaitic analysis on two points. First, Advaitins claim that mind and the modifications that intend toward objects are physical in nature. Second, Advaitins neither limit consciousness to intentional activity nor deny unconscious mental traces in accounting for habit and memory.

In spite of these differences, which also serve as points of distinction between Husserl and Advaita, it is clear that Brentano's conception of intentionality does share with the Advaitic conception the desire to insure direct contact between the subject and external objects. But it is precisely in overturning this point and reversing Brentano's claim to be able to investigate objects in their own right that Husserl's so-called betrayal of the original spirit of intentionality is said to lie. Specifically, by arguing

1. G. Berger, *Le Cogito dans la philosophie de Husserl,* (Paris, 1941), p. 96, quoted in Gurwitsch, *Field*, p. 183.

2. Sartre, *op. cit.*, translator's introduction, p. 18.

3. Cf. discussion in Spiegelberg, *op. cit.*, pp. 39-42

that real objects transcend the intentional act, Husserl succeeds in driving a wedge not only between the conscious act and the real object but also between the act and the ideal object. And once he has established this new realm of ideal entities, Husserl can undertake a much more complex analysis of intentionality itself. Thus intentionality is no longer the direct "reference to an object" of Brentano's conscious act. Rather, it indicates the identifying and connecting functions that enable acts of consciousness to originate or constitute ideal objects. And along with the more complex analysis of the synthesizing function of mind which this constitutive activity of consciousness affords comes the idealistic account of perceptual experience that is in direct opposition to the realistic Advaitic description of both intentional consciousness and waking experience as a whole.

Husserl's doctrine of intentional consciousness is thus more complex than that of Advaita, and its complexity itself reflects the aims of a philosophical tradition very different from that of Advaita. In fact, these differences are at times so great that we find that intentionality is for Husserl the phenomenon in terms of which correct knowledge of the world, or freedom, is attained, while for Advaita intentionality is the process through which man loses himself in the bondage of the world.

Dream Consciousness

As stated previously, the Advaitin characterizes the second level of consciousness, or dream experience, in terms of the awareness of interior mental life as presented to the individual in the form of subtle dream objects. In this sense individual dream consciousness is withdrawn from the world of external objects and from the "self-forgetfulness" that accompanies the waking level of experience. Nevertheless, the dreamer does remain involved in the causal or karmic order as a result of his identification with, and enjoyment of, dream content. For this reason the consciousness manifest in the dream state is bound, just as it was in waking experience. At the same time, however, we have argued that dream experience represents a relatively greater degree of autonomy of consciousness because the self, even though under the influence of ignorance and desire, creates and illumines the content of which it is aware. But we have also acknowledged that the increased autonomy and creativity of consciousness evident in dream experience makes sense only from the subjective hierarchical perspective, and that the Upaniṣads as well as Advaitic thinkers alternate between this and the objective perspective depending upon the particular context in which they introduce and analyse dream phenomena.

We can abstract from this point and make a general remark concerning the nature of dream analysis in the Advaitic tradition as well as in Indian thought as a whole. That is, the tradition has usually come to address the study of dreams in the context of the analysis and defense of some other issue, whether it be the nature of error, perception, magic or, as in our present case, consciousness and reality. Furthermore, the perspective in terms of which these issues were treated also varied, from psychology and physiology to philosophy and spirituality. Thus, we find that both individual thinkers and schools of thought often subscribed to more than one analysis of dream phenomena, depending upon such factors as the context of the discussion, the position of an opponent and, indeed, the complexity and intangibility of dreams themselves. In fact, six general analyses of the nature and origin of dreams were presented in classical Indian thought, and it is clear that Śaṅkara and his followers upheld, in one context or another, at least five of these six.[1] In order to discover just what Advaitins mean when they talk about the dream state, then, we must present both a general description as well as the Advaitic interpretation of each of these classical Indian analyses of the nature of dream.

The first account of the nature and origin of dreams has been called the "presentative" theory because its proponents treat dreams as a kind of positive perception, rather than as a form of memory or recollection, consisting in the direct and immediate presentation of an object to the mind.[2] These theorists argue that the objects of dream-cognition are actively produced by the mind in response, for example, to certain internal physiological changes, from subconscious impressions (*saṁskāra*) based on past experience rather than from the present activity of the external sense organs. In this sense the resemblance between dream

1. Cf. J. Sinha, *Indian Psychology — Perception*, pp. 306-323; Krishna Das Gupta, *The Shadow World*, pp. 51-83.

2. Sinha, *op. cit.*, pp. 306-308.

and waking consists in the fact that in both cases the mind is active in the formation of vivid, direct perceptions, although the increased activity of mind in the dream state is accompanied by the objective invalidity of its content.

The most obvious instance of a presentative analysis of dreams to be found in the Advaitic tradition is contained in the *Vedāntaparibhāṣā*. In this work Dharmarāja treats the dream experience as a kind of direct, non-sense-generated perception resulting from the activity of the mind. He argues that these perceptions are defective or delusive and must therefore be included in a discussion of the Advaitic analysis of error.[1] Some of Śaṅkara's remarks on the nature of dreams have been interpreted to indicate that he too was open to an analysis in terms of the presentative model, although, as will be made clear in the subsequent discussion, he usually used other models to account for this level of experience. In his commentary on Gauḍapāda's discussion of illusion, for example, Śaṅkara says that we have direct perception of objects in dreams, such as mountains and elephants, brought about by mental activity although these objects are false, i.e., not objective, precisely because they are located in the mind.[2] Again, in his commentary on the *Bṛhadāraṇyaka Upaniṣad*, Śaṅkara argues that the individual creates ("becomes the light" of) the objects of dream perception through the stimulation of subtle past impressions.[3]

It is important to note that part of the significance attached to treating dream as a kind of perception lies in emphasizing the reality, i.e., the directness and immediacy, involved in the dream experience itself. In other words, while the content of dream experience is false, this same content is nevertheless experienced with the vivacity, immediacy and certainty that characterizes waking, intentional perception. Thus, Śaṅkara argues that although the dream content, e.g., seeing oneself flying through space, is contradicted upon waking, the dream experience itself remains an empirically real fact, i.e., one has actually dreamed that one flew through space. Śaṅkara concludes two important points from this. First, he maintains that the content of dreams

1. *Vedāntaparibhāṣā* 1.108, 110, 115.
2. *Gauḍapāda Kārikā S.B.* 2.1.
2. *Bṛhad. S.B.* 4.3.10; Das Gupta, *op. cit.*, pp. 69-70.

is as consistent in its own sphere as waking content is to the waking subject, since dream content is only sublated or contradicted upon waking.[1] The fact that dream is incongruous with waking and waking is, likewise, incompatible with dream, establishes that the two spheres are discontinuous from each other, and that each is equally autonomous in its own domain. In this sense, Śaṅkara offers an implicit rejection of Descartes' attempt, in the *Sixth Meditation,* to distinguish waking from dreaming on the basis of the claim that the former is more consistent than the latter. Second, Śaṅkara maintains that dream perceptual experience is as real, in terms of phenomenal consciousness, as waking perceptual experience but that ultimately both are bound and illusory.[2] And in this sense Śaṅkara extends the discussion of philosophically relevant experience beyond the waking state and its conditions.

The second theory in terms of which Advaitins describe the nature of dream experience emphasizes the reproductive function of memory as the cause of dreams. Professor Sinha has called this the "representative" theory of dreams because it claims that dream content consists in a recollection of some previously perceived external object in the form of a subconscious impression (*saṁskāra*) or representation left by that object in the mind.[3] Using this model to distinguish dream from waking experience, Śaṅkara says that "what we experience in dreams is due to memory, while what we experience in waking life is immediate apprehension [of external objects]."[4] And he seems to indicate that this model offers an adequate description of the nature of most dreams when he says "a dream is not an entirely new experience, for most often it is the memory of past experiences."[5]

It is clear, however, that certain dream content cannot be accounted for in terms of the literal reproduction of waking impressions, e.g., pink elephants or men flying through space. In order to explain these types of dream experiences, Advaitins introduce the notion of the mind's capacity for creativity or constructive imagination (*kalpanā*) based upon the impressions

1. *Chand. S.B.* 8.5.4.
2. *Gauḍapāda Kārikā S.B.* 2.5.
3. Sinha, *op. cit.*, pp. 308-309.
4. *B.S.S.B.* 2.2.29.
5. *Bṛhad. S.B.* 4.3.9.

supplied by memory. And in this context Śaṅkara asserts that the greater freedom demonstrated by consciousness in creating the objects and conditions of, and the emotional response to, its dream experience indicates that consciousness is actually more detached from its content in this state. Thus consciousness is not only involved in the creation of, but is also the witness to, dream experience. Further, Śaṅkara argues that the fact that consciousness witnesses its dreams means that consciousness reveals or illumines them. Indeed, without the aid of the external senses and physical light, what other than the light of consciousness itself illumines dream objects ?[1] In other words, beginning with the creativity and detachment of dream consciousness from its content, Śaṅkara argues both for the continuity of self-awareness throughout the various states of experience as well as for the self-luminosity of consciousness itself. In this way Śaṅkara attaches great metaphysical significance to the analysis of dream experience in general, and to the point that dream objects are the creation of the mind in particular. Indeed, he says that "By the illustration of dreams it has been proved that there is the self-luminous Ātman, and that it transcends the forms of death [i.e., is eternal]"[2]

While the presentative and reproductive theories emphasize, respectively, the role of the sense-mind (*manas*) and memory (*citta*) aspects of mind (*antaḥkaraṇa*) in the production of dreams, our next theory introduces a volitional, discriminative element in its account which can be associated with the reason-intellect (*buddhi*) aspect of mind. This third theory maintains that dreams constitute the fulfillment of desires. In general terms, this account is based on the claim that desires (*vāsanā*) acquire the strength to motivate the construction of dream content from among subconscious impressions when the external sense-organs are inactive. Quoting from the Upaniṣads, "He who desires, dreams; he who does not desire does not dream."[3] In the context of Advaitic thought these wish-fulfillment dreams are a result of the activity (*karman*) of the mind which is conditioned by desire (*kāma*) or attachment based on ignorance. Thus, Śaṅkara

1. *Bṛhad. S.B.* 4.3.9; 4.3.14; *B.S.S.B.* 3.2.4.
2. *Bṛhad. S.B.* 4.3.14.
3. *Bṛhad. Up.* 3.3.19.

says that "the individual soul ... after the cessation in sleep of the senses, creates a subtle body of desires, and shapes the dreams according to the light of his buddhi."[1]

A distinctive feature of wish-fulfillment dreams, according to Advaita, is that they are retributive, i.e., they reflect and provide, to some extent, a measure of one's attachment and confusion. In fact, Śaṅkara goes so far as to say that "the creation in the dream . . . is for the purpose of causing joy and fear to the dreamer in accordance with his good or bad deeds."[2] In this sense, Śaṅkara argues that ignorance and desire motivate various painful and pleasant dream cognitions.[3] He explains that desires can manifest in the form of painful and pleasurable dream cognitions because dreams are one type of mental activity and are therefore produced by desires themselves, i.e., what the individual desires, he resolves and what he resolves, he works out.[4] Thus Śaṅkara maintains that the general condition of the individual's sub-conscious impressions parallels the moral quality of the individual's waking activity and experience. We will point out subsequently that this position is exactly opposite to what Jung calls the compensatory function of the unconscious as it manifests in dreams.

In addition to the retributive function associated with wish-fulfilling dreams, Śaṅkara, following the Indian tradition, maintains that dreams can also be prophetic or veridical. In the case of this fourth type of dream analysis the tradition argues that the individual's good and bad deeds (*dharma* and *adharma*) actually cause auspicious and inauspicious dreams respectively. In affirming this theory, Śaṅkara even takes the trouble to list a number of typically prophetic dreams and the various events they portend.[5] Note the common assumption underlying the wish-fulfillment and prophetic theories of dream : the destructive or negative desires and the evil deeds (*adharma*) which these desires prompt not only cause painful and inauspicious dreams but they actually cause these dreams to come true. Thus, these two dream theories presuppose that there is some principle of moral justice

1. *B.S.S.B.* 3.2.4.
2. *B.S.S.B.* 3.2.4.
3. *Chand. S.B.* 6.8.1.
4. *Bṛhad. S.B.* 4.4.5.
5. *B.S.S.B.* 3.2.4.

at work in the universe. This principle is, of course, the law of *karman*.

This survey of the Advaitic interpretation of classical Indian dream theories can be completed by dealing with the remaining two analyses in a cursory manner. The fifth theory, which describes telepathic dreams, does not appear to have been taken into consideration by Advaitic thinkers and the sixth, which describes the phenomena known as "dreams-within-dreams" is categorized by Advaitins as a variety of representative type dreams, discussed above.[1]

Our understanding of the Advaitic analysis of dream consciousness can be broadened by contrasting it with the dream theories offered by the Western thinkers Sigmund Freud and C. G. Jung. Specifically, the Advaitic discussion of the importance of wish-fulfillment as a cause of dreams suggests an immediate similarity with Freud's well-known thesis. Further, many of the conclusions regarding the nature of consciousness which the Advaitin draws from his analysis of dreams are reflected in interesting ways in Jung's treatment of the relationship between dreams and the psyche.

Turning first to Freud's analysis of dreams, we immediately observe the central importance that Freud attaches both to the concept of wish-fulfillment and to the process by which wish-fulfillment motivates the production of dreams. Indeed, Freud's in-depth treatment of the details associated with this theory is necessitated by the fact that he wants to argue that wish-fulfillment is the sole motivation for all dreams. Claiming that "In every dream an instinctual wish has to be represented as fulfilled,"[2] Freud concludes that this phenomenon is the universal characteristic of all dreams, providing the key to their explanation.[3] Furthermore, he argues that the process, called "dream-work," through which an unconscious wish creates a dream, has ramifications which extend beyond the study of the dream phenomenon itself and can serve as a model for both the study of the

1. Cf. Sinha, *op. cit.*, pp. 320-321; Das Gupta, *op. cit.*, pp. 79-81 for more complete discussion.

2. Sigmund Freud, *New Introductory Lectures on Psychoanalysis*, pp. 18-19. (Hereafter : *Lectures*).

3. Sigmund Freud, *A General Introduction to Psychoanalysis*, p. 118. (Hereafter : *Introduction*).

formation of all types of neurotic symptoms and the development of man's faculties of speech and thought.[1] Certainly, Freud places a much greater emphasis on the concept of wish-fulfillment than did Advaitins.

Freud maintains that dreams are composed of the remnants of the mental activity of waking experience, and as such have the potential to disturb dreamless sleep, a state which is biologically and psychologically necessary for recuperation from the demands of waking experience, and is best when not disturbed by any mental stimuli at all.[2] Thus Freud argues that dreams function to remove, via wish-fulfillment, potentially disturbing mental stimuli.[3] It is clear, however, that a disturbing mental stimulus can be removed by the gratification of a wish only if that stimulus is caused by a frustrated or unfulfilled wish. And this is precisely Freud's point, for he wants to argue that these stimuli or unconscious impulses are actually instincts or untamed passions which demand satisfaction but which have been repressed, according to the censorship of the super-ego, by the ego in its struggle to relate successfully with the external world, i.e., with physical, social and cultural demands. Of course, Freud does not want to limit the unconscious material or latent dream-thoughts drawn upon in dream-work to repressed unconscious wish-impulses. It is in this context that he introduces the role of memory in the guise of "the residue from the previous day" in contributing material for dream formation, but he insists that this formation is possible only as a result of a repressed wish-impulse.[4]

Once Freud has provided an account of the reasons why latent dream-thoughts take up residence in the unconscious, he proceeds with his explanation of the dream-work, i.e., the theoretical model for the transformation of the latent into the manifest dream. While this type of account is lacking in Advaitic thought, it would seem to correspond to what the Advaitin might suggest if he were to try to explain how constructive imagination (*kalpanā*) interacts with desire to create a dream. However,

1. Cf. Freud's discussion of this point in *Introduction, op. cit.*, 158-162.
2. *Ibid.*, pp. 79-80.
3. *Ibid.*, p. 190.
4. *Ibid.*, p. 202.

since the Advaitin does not enter into as elaborate a discussion of the repression and censorship of desires as does Freud (although some mechanism like repression would not be incompatible with the Advaitic position), the Advaitin is not committed to as detailed an interpretation of how dream symbols are distorted manifestations of wish-fulfillment as is Freud.

For Freud, then, the dream-work is a fourfold process through which repressed wishes are transformed into reality and latent thoughts into visual dream images.[1] The first aspect of this process is called condensation, referring to the abbreviation of the richness and range of latent thoughts in the manifest dream. Condensation has the effect of blending a number of different latent thoughts together in a somewhat blurred and obscure way so that it becomes impossible to distinguish a direct correspondence between latent and manifest dream content. The next aspect, called displacement, has the effect of distorting the dream content in a manner pleasing to the censor. This takes place in two ways : by substituting an allusion for a latent thought; and by shifting the accent of a dream from the central to a peripheral point. A third aspect, called plastic representation, refers to the transformation of latent thoughts and of the relationships between them into visual images and helps to explain the way various symbols emerge in dream experience. Finally, Freud discusses secondary elaboration or the mechanism by which the results of the dream-work are brought together into a coherent but totally misleading dream manifestation.

In spite of Freud's attempt to use his theory of dream-work to explain how wish-fulfillment is distorted in the very process of motivating dreams, he nevertheless has great difficulty in accounting for painful emotional dreams, e.g., dreams of anxiety and punishment. This problem provides an interesting point of comparison between Freudian and Advaitic theories concerning wish-fulfilling dreams. In order for Freud to reconcile the claim that dreams gratify wishes with the experience of painful dreams, he is forced to argue that the censoring agency called the super-ego has managed to infiltrate the unconscious. Thus, dreams of punishment represent attempts to fulfill the wishes of

1. Cf. discussion in *Introduction, op. cit.*, pp. 151-162; *Lectures, op. cit.*, pp. 19-22; Sigmund Freud, *The Interpretation of Dreams*, pp. 174-366.

the unconscious super-ego, while anxiety results when a repressed wish is so openly fulfilled in a dream that it causes great pain to the censor.[1] If nothing else, this resolution of the problem in question shows that Freud's self is a battleground with different forces waging heated conflict among each other. Furthermore, while this battle can be brought under control through psychotherapy, the conflict cannot be eliminated altogether since it is part of what it means to be a human being.

On the other hand, as we have seen, Advaitins argue that some desires are evil in the sense that they represent negative, harmful individual conditioning (*adharma*). These desires may be accompanied by pain as a result of the operation of the universal moral law. In this sense, Śaṅkara argues in opposition to Freud that the subconscious desires which motivate many dreams express themselves accurately and directly in those dreams. Further, Śaṅkara would reject Freud's reduction of the principle of moral retribution to the operation of the super-ego in conjunction with plastic representation.[2] Part of the basis upon which Śaṅkara argues these points consists in the fact that Advaitins do not see an interminable conflict between the id's instincts and the super-ego's repression, or between pleasure and control, as does Freud. Rather, Advaitins argue that one can bring one's desires into harmony with the universal moral order in preparation for the transcendence of both desire and the moral order. Thus the Advaitin argues that a man who has realized Brahman can be free from the conflict between the pleasure-principle and the censor, i.e., he can be "in the world but not of it."

While the theory that wish-fulfillment motivates the production of dreams suggests a specific and significant point of similarity between Freudian and Advaitic treatments of the dream experience, we find that many of the conclusions concerning the nature of absolute consciousness which are drawn by the Advaitin from his analysis of dream phenomena parallel some of the conclusions regarding the nature of the collective unconscious that Jung draws based upon his analysis of dreams. That is,

1. Cf. *Lectures, op. cit.*, pp. 27-28; *Introduction, op. cit.*, pp. 192-193.
2. Cf. Freud's discussion of "Divine Retribution" in *Lectures, op. cit.*, p. 156.

both the Advaitin and Jung argue that in dreams we are confronted with the greater autonomy, creativity and potential for fully satisfying renewal which characterize absolute consciousness and the collective unconscious respectively. Of course, a number of important differences accompany these similarities and will also be mentioned in the following remarks.

Jung defines dream as an apperceptual or psychic process, as opposed to a sensory and physiological one, which is irrational, fragmentary, analogical and logically discontinuous in character.[1] Because dreams occur naturally and spontaneously as the result of unconscious processes obtruding on consciousness, Jung argues that dreams are the most readily accessible expression of these processes and provide us with a self-portrait of psychic life.[2] In elaborating the nature of unconscious processes, however, Jung distinguishes between the personal and collective unconscious and at once incorporates, and moves beyond, Freud. Jung's personal unconscious is composed of content that has been acquired through individual experience but which has since become unconscious as a result of loss of memory, repression or not having had sufficient intensity to reach consciousness but having been assimilated nevertheless. Thus Jung provides a causal account for the content of the individual unconscious, following Freud, and further notes, again in accordance with his teacher, that the release of these repressed wishes, memories, tendencies, plans, etc., to consciousness in dream analysis, for example, is usually unpleasant.[3]

In presenting his theory of the collective unconscious, however, Jung breaks irrevocably with Freud. For Jung, the content of the collective unconscious is not acquired but comprises an inherited and universal psychic disposition which is "born anew in the brain structure of every individual."[4] This content

1. C. G. Jung, "The Structure of the Psyche" in *The Portable Jung*, ed. by Joseph Campbell (New York : Penguin, 1977), pp. 25-27. (Hereafter : *Portable*).

2. *Ibid.*, p. 29; C. G. Jung, "The Transcendent Function" in *Portable, op. cit.*, p. 283; C. G. Jung, *Dreams* (Princeton : Bollingen Series, 1974), p. 49.

3. C. G. Jung, *Two Essays on Analytic Psychology* (New York : Bollingen, 1953), pp. 133-134 (Hereafter : *Two Essays*); *Portable, op. cit.*, p. 38.

4. *Portable, op. cit.*, p. 45.

serves a universal psychic nature which is independent of individual needs. And as examples of this autonomy and creativity, Jung points to dreams involving spatio-temporal distortion or contradiction of the rational order imposed on experience by the unconscious mind.[1] Furthermore, Jung argues that this autonomous, inherited content consists in primordial images or thought-patterns, called archetypes, which can exercise power over, and effect radical and unforeseen changes in, the conscious mind. In this sense the content of the collective unconscious is not only independent of the conscious mind, but it actively opposes, with irrationality and chaos, the resistance or inability of the rational, conscious mind to come to terms with some barrier to the psyche's movement towards wholeness or individuation. Again, dreams manifest this conflict in the psyche as it is actually occurring, thus providing us with additional demonstrations of the autonomy and creativity of the collective unconscious.[2]

Two points of significance for our present discussion emerge from these remarks. The first is that while dream experience is used by both the Advaitin and Jung to establish the autonomous and contradictory nature of absolute consciousness or universal psychic reality with respect to waking consciousness, we should not assume that the Advaitin's pure consciousness is identical with Jung's collective unconscious. The fact is that both Jung and the Advaitin are forced to try to point to the more universal level of psychic or conscious reality precisely because this reality is not directly knowable in, and is contradictory to, waking consciousness.[3] Similarly, in spite of the fact that both Jung and the Advaitin use their autonomous levels to account for radical changes of consciousness, we ought not conclude that these changes are similar. That is, while Jung uses the structure and activity of the collective unconscious as an hypothesis which accounts for pathological states of mind,[4] the only radical change of consciousness the Advaitin admits is one whic involves transcendental, undifferentiated knowledge. Further,

1. *Two Essays, op. cit.*, pp. 158-159.
2. *Ibid.*, pp. 107-109.
3. *Ibid.*, 175.
4. *Portable, op. cit.*, p. 28.

Jung's universal psychic reality is structured by the heritage of aeons of human and even animal evolution,[1] while for Advaitins absolute consciousness transcends karmic and evolutionary activity altogether.

Beyond accounting for pathological episodes, however, Jung's collective unconscious represents the storehouse of wisdom accumulated through mankind's past efforts to come to terms with the meaning of life. In this sense, Jung argues that the collective unconscious functions teleologically in striving to present its wisdom concerning the progressive stages of human experience to man at the appropriate transitions in life when this wisdom can serve to guide him towards his potential perfection or individuation, i.e., creative and whole living in the world.[2] And this, of course, is contrary to the Advaitic notion that the goal of human life entails the transcendence of the stages of life (*āśrama*) and the phenomenal world itself.

The second point to be discussed in this context is that the opposition which the content of dreams offers to individual conscious experience is, for Jung, one of the ways that the teleological activity of the collective unconscious can manifest. In other words, Jung is arguing that the psyche as a whole is a "self-regulating system" and that the success of its regulatory activity requires the collective unconscious to oppose conscious content and thereby to guide man to increased self-realization.[3] And the place where this opposition is most evident, he concludes, is in our dreams. For this reason Jung claims that the dream content, which reveals its meaning directly and non-deceptively, complements rather than parallels the content of waking experience. (Of course, Jung emphasizes that dreams are symbolic in nature and, thus, the proper understanding of the meaning of a dream requires symbolic interpretation.) He refers to this complementary opposition as the "compensatory relationship" between the unconscious and conscious layers of the psyche.[4]

1. *Two Essays*, *op. cit.*, pp. 96-97. Cf. p. 76, where Jung specifically acknowledges his debt to the Indian concept of *karma* in the formulation of this aspect of his theory.
2. *Ibid.*, pp. 96-97, 114, 128, 182; *Dreams*, *op. cit.*, pp. 27-29.
3. *Portable*, *op. cit.*, pp. 273-4, 285, 287-8.
4. *Dreams*, *op. cit.*, pp. 36-37; *Two Essays*, *op. cit.*, pp. 107-108. We should mention at this point that Jung also acknowledges a "prospective" function of dreams, which he describes as "an anticipation in the unconscious of future conscious achievements," and which is not unlike the Advaitin's prophetic or veridical type dream. Cf. *Dreams*, pp. 41-42.

Further, Jung argues that, to the extent that dreams have the capacity to rectify a psychic imbalance, an understanding of their meaning can help to educate man and guide him toward wholeness. Thus, while Jung's compensatory function is somewhat akin to the retributive nature of dreams posited by Advaitins, Jung does not limit the importance of this function to the understanding of the moral condition of, or the possible imbalance in, the psyche as do the latter. Rather, it is clear that the theoretical analysis of dreams as manifestations of the autonomy, creativity and radical discontinuity of the collective unconscious suggests a much greater role for practical dream interpretation in the spiritual work of Jungian therapy than the parallel analysis of the nature of dream experience does for the Advaitic spiritual path.

Deep Sleep Consciousness

The third hierarchical level distinguished by Advaitins in their analysis of consciousness is the experience of deep sleep. In opposition to the duality which characterizes waking and dreaming, this state is said to consist in the temporary identification of the individual self (*jīva*) with Ātman which results from the cessation of the mutual superimposition of the Self and not-Self. Following the Upaniṣadic analysis of sleep, Advaitins explain that this suspension takes place because the activity of the gross and subtle bodies, i.e., of the external sense organs and mind, ceases to operate in this state. In other words, sleep is the temporary interruption of the projecting and differentiating activity which arises as a result of the limitations imposed upon the Self by ignorance. In the absence of this limiting activity the *jīva* is embraced by, and becomes one with, the Self, assuming what the texts like to describe as a knowing or witnessing attitude in which objects are undifferentiated and nothing is known.[1] That is, in deep sleep the limitations imposed by *avidyā* and constituting the content of waking and dream experience, e.g., space, time and causality, desire and karmic activity, are in a latent or potential condition. Thus, there is nothing for the individual in its witnessing attitude to confront beyond inactive *avidyā* itself. For this reason the deep sleep state is described as a thick mass of unified consciousness (*prajñānaghana*) in

1. *Bṛhad. Up.* 4.3.23.

which the content of waking and dream experience has coalesced.[1] Dreamless sleep is said to consist in the non-apprehension of illusion or, more positively, in the consciousness of pure, potential *avidyā*, i.e., of primal, blank objectivity.[2]

While Advaitins thus maintain that deep sleep is an undifferentiated or non-dual state based on the absence of mental activity, they reject the suggestion that it is an unconscious state, i.e., one in which there is a loss of consciousness. Rather, they insist not only that sleep is a conscious experience but that it has the phenomenological characteristic of bliss (*ānanda*) as well. Advaitins offer two justifications for their position. The first is based on scriptural testimony. For example, the *Māṇḍūkya Upaniṣad* claims that deep sleep is full of the experience of bliss.[3] Further, the *Bṛhadāraṇyaka Upaniṣad* says that sleep is the experience of highest serenity (*samprasāda*), bringing with it greater joy than can be found in the waking or dream states.[4] Sleep, this text continues, is an experience which is beyond all suffering and fear, which is free from desire and grief. It is an experience of unqualified, incalculable happiness and well-being, of harmony and integration accompanying the loss of individual consciousness and all its concerns in the identification with absolute consciousness, i.e., in the embrace of the Supreme Self.[5]

The second justification is based on the Advaitin's claim to have a reflective cognition or memory of blissful sleep experience upon waking. The Advaitin argues on the one hand that it would be absurd for him to try to claim that he perceives the blissful experience of sleep while it takes place, since he has already claimed that the senses and the other means of knowledge are inactive in this state. On the other hand, however, he argues that the immediate awareness of the blissful nature of sleep experience realized when we awaken cannot derive from an inference based on contrasting our memory of having been in a state of disquieted knowledge prior to sleep with the peacefulness accompanying waking.[6] He thus concludes that the blissful

1. *Māṇḍūkya Up. S.B.* 1.5.
2. Bhattacharyya, *op. cit.*, p. 19.
3. *Māṇḍūkya Up.* 1.5.
4. *Bṛhad. Up. S.B.* 4.3.15.
5. *Bṛhad. Up. S.B.* 4.3.21.
6. Bhattacharyya, *op. cit.*, pp. 18-19.

absence of suffering was actually revealed or presented in sleep, although it was not perceived as such until the knowing mind was reactivated upon waking.

This phenomenological analysis of the deep sleep state is extremely important for the Advaitin, for it is in terms of this analysis that he argues for the non-dual, self-luminous and, as we have seen in a previous chapter,[1] the blissful nature of pure consciousness. It may seem somewhat odd to a person trained in Western philosophy that an analysis of dreamless sleep should play a significant role in the philosophical defense of a particular theory of consciousness. Of course, both Freud and Jung saw in sleep a physiologically and psychologically necessary period of relief and recovery from the strains of waking experience, a point that goes back at least as far as Aristotle,[2] but there seems to be little of philosophical concern for these thinkers behind this observation. On the other hand, while Śaṅkara discusses the physiology of sleep and acknowledges its value in allowing the individual to recover from fatigue,[3] he goes beyond this and extracts arguments for his theory of Self from his discussion of sleep. And he is not alone among Indian philosophers in doing this.

For example, Śaṅkara claims that the undifferentiated, distinctionless nature of sleep experience demonstrates the true, non-dual nature of the consciousness which persists throughout, and remains unaffected by, all three phenomenal states. After offering a series of arguments to show there is continuity of self-identity between deep sleep and the dreaming and waking states,[4] Śaṅkara concludes that we get a glimpse of the non-dual nature of this persistent consciousness in deep sleep, which is a natural state, free from effort, struggle, relationship to another and the limitations of ignorance.[5] In other words, the blissful absence of duality in sleep reveals the non-dual nature of absolute consciousness itself. Rāmānuja found this point unacceptable, insisting instead that there is some differentiated

1. Cf. Chapter II, above, for arguments for bliss.
2. Cf. Aristotle, *Parva Naturalia* 454a-454b.
3. *Bṛhad. Up. S.B.* 4.3.19; *B.S.S.B.* 3.2.7.
4. *B.S.S.B.* 3.2.9.
5. *Māṇḍūkya Up. S.B.* 1.6; *Gauḍapāda Kārikā S.B.* 1.6.1.

awareness, however slight, of individual, ego consciousness in deep sleep.[1] And this, of course, was in support of Rāmānuja's claim that individual self-awareness is the essential nature of consciousness itself.

Similarly, deep sleep plays an important part in the debate concerning the self-luminosity of consciousness. The Advaitin is committed to the doctrine of the essential luminosity of the Self as well as the claim that nothing is perceived or known in the sleep state. His opponents object, however, that these two positions are contradictory since a state in which nothing is perceived or known is actually an unconscious state, i.e., a state in which luminous consciousness is absent.[2] Śaṅkara counters this objection by claiming that the absence of knowledge in deep sleep is a consequence of the absence of anything experienced separate from consciousness, rather than the absence of consciousness itself.[3] Furthermore, he argues that the blissful nature of sleep experience can only be explained as a presentation of self-luminous consciousness to itself, since all other modes of awareness are in their latent condition.

In the course of elaborating his analysis of deep sleep, however, Śaṅkara was confronted with an additional and somewhat more perplexing objection. Granting that sleep is in fact an experience of blissful, self-luminous consciousness, how can the Advaitin account for such blatantly unconscious states as coma, fainting and being "knocked out" ? If these states actually represent a loss of consciousness, then not only is Śaṅkara's doctrine of persistent, self-luminous awareness thrown into serious doubt, but his claim to provide a comprehensive description of phenomenal experience in terms of the waking, dream and sleep states is undermined as well. Clearly, the problem presented to Śaṅkara in this context involves the question of just what a phenomenal or life experience is, and at just what point life experience itself ends and death begins. In fact, this is a question with respect to which physicians, lawyers and ethicists are still very much in conflict today.

Śaṅkara's not altogether satisfactory answer to this question

1. *Śri Bhāṣya* 1.1.1.

2. *Śāstradīpikā*, p. 352, quoted in Saksena, *op. cit.*, p. 114.

3. *Bṛhad Up. S.B.* 4.3.23.

consists in maintaining that there is partial agreement between these various unconscious conditions and both deep sleep and death.[1] These conditions are both superficially similar to sleep, in the sense that both represent an absence of waking and dream consciousness, and to death, in the sense that people frequently pass away after having been in these states for some time. On the other hand, Śaṅkara has to confess that there is not much real similarity between these conditions and either sleep or death, since the causes, physiological and phenomenological characteristics, etc., which distinguish unconsciousness from both sleep and death are quite great. Śaṅkara concludes his discussion by conceding that we ought to grant these states a status of their own, although they occur relatively rarely and by implication, perhaps, are not very central to his theory of consciousness.

Aside from this issue, another apparent inconsistency connected with Śaṅkara's analysis of deep sleep must be clarified. It is quite frequently the case that Upaniṣadic and Advaitic descriptions of deep sleep seem to identify it with determinate reality (*saguṇa Brahman*) itself. For example, the *Māṇḍūkya Upaniṣad* asserts that sleep is the Lord (*Īśvara*) of all, the knower of all, the source and controller of all.[2] And *Īśvara,* or Brahman with the attributes existence, knowledge and bliss, is said to correspond phenomenologically with the spiritual state of harmonious, loving, unified being (*savikalpa samādhi*, *bhakti*) which is an experience of transcendental and not phenomenal consciousness. The problem with these identifications is that they seem to equate the deep sleep state with spiritual experience in such a way that the former no longer represents a bound and limited level of consciousness. But no one, including Śaṅkara himself, would want to claim either that sleep is a transcendental experience or that it affects the individual in the way we would expect a complete spiritual experience to affect an individual.

Advaitins make clear, however, that this identification between

1. *B.S.S.B.* 3.2.10. Note that Śaṅkara fails to treat death as a level of conscious experience. One wonders why Śaṅkara does not try to use even death to support his argument for the persistence of consciousness by drawing, for example, upon traditional statements indicating that death itself is followed by consciousness, either in terms of rebirth into the phenomenal world or in terms of liberation.

2. *Māṇḍūkya Up.* 1.6.

blissful deep sleep and loving, harmonious, non-dual spiritual experience is not a total one.[1] Rather, it is a negative identification based on the common absence of suffering and dualistic cognitive awareness which both sleep and determinate (*savikalpa*) spiritual experience share. From a more positive perspective, though, the identification breaks down at a number of points. First, the absence of suffering and of dualistic awareness in sleep occurs as a result of dispersion or loss of mental attention and the consequent isolation of the individual self from internal and external objects. On the other hand, the non-dual, blissful awareness of *savikalpa samādhi* results from intense concentration of attention on an object of devotion, e.g., *Īśvara*, so that the individual is unified with reality or the "other". In other words, the awareness of relationship is suspended in deep sleep, while in *samādhi* a "duality in unity"[2] is presented which harmonizes relations. Second, upon awakening from sleep, the individual has no knowledge of anything and merely remembers that he experienced a blissful absence of duality. Upon the cessation of *samādhi*, however, the individual is aware of having been unified with reality, i.e., he has positive knowledge of the fullness of being which unites all distinctions. But the fact that both of these experiences come to an end in time makes an additional aspect of the identification between sleep and *samādhi* clear. That is, Advaitins identify both of these as causal states because they contain the latent seeds of future activity and of discriminating knowledge which emerge with the cessation of each state.

The third reason that the identification fails to apply, then, is that deep sleep, with its absence of knowledge, confronts but never breaks through ignorance (*avidyā*) and the seeds of future bondage contained therein, while the loving awareness of *bhakti* actually bursts through the barrier of ignorance and transforms the seeds of duality with positive knowledge of reality. Thus, the deep sleep experience remains a phenomenal, bound and causal condition, while *savikalpa samādhi* transforms bondage into love. The Advaitin nevertheless denies that this harmonious

1. Cf. excellent discussion of this point in Bhattacharyya, *op. cit.*, pp. 26-29.

2. Deutsch, *op. cit.*, p. 13.

and blissful *bhakti* experience is equivalent to the highest spiritual realization (*nirvikalpa samādhi*) precisely because the former consists in the unification of all distinctions and causes while the latter entails their complete transcendence or sublation. For this reason the Advaitin argues that loving, blissful experience represents a transitional phase to the highest freedom, but one which fails to completely cancel the causal order and the mutual superimposition of real and non-real.[1] We note in passing that this issue became one of the major points of contention between Advaitins and Indian theists. That is, while Śaṅkara considers *bhakti* (and *karma*) *yoga* as preliminary and inferior to the path of knowledge, Rāmānuja, for example, elevates *bhakti* as the primary means to, and expression of, salvation. Thus, the parallel drawn by the Advaitin between deep sleep and the state of devotion, corresponding to his relegation of divine love and personal God, is seen as a gross distortion of the nature of reality by theists such as Rāmānuja.

Clearly, then, Advaitins are using deep sleep consciousness as an analogy for one of the most fundamental and universal of spiritual experiences, whether it be called a feeling of love, harmony, bliss, devotion or a sense of wholeness and well-being. And in light of what has been said about Rāmānuja's objection to this comparison, one is not surprised that the use of sleep as the analogy for blissful, harmonious and loving experience in the Advaitic tradition contrasts most strikingly with the way this type of experience is portrayed in many other philosophical, religious and even literary contexts, especially in those influenced by some form of theism. For in these latter cases the experience of bliss is presented in terms of the analogy of love, most typically symbolized by the divine union between the soul of the religious aspirant and God. In the Medieval Christian tradition, for example, a number of saints speak of deification or a mystical union (*unio mystica*) which seems similar phenomenologically to the Advaitic *savikalpa samādhi* except perhaps for the fact that the Christian experience is more emotionally charged. For these Christians, deification refers to an ecstatic experience in which the soul and God are united with no awareness of distinction

1. The subject of freedom in Advaita is treated in more detail in the following section of this chapter.

remaining. Using the idea of love to talk about this blissful union with God, St. John of the Cross says :

What peace, with love enwreathing,
You conjure to my breast
Which only you your dwelling place may call :
While the delicious breathings
In glory, grace and rest,
So delicately in love you make me fall ![1]

And with respect to the surrender of the individual ego which accompanies this ecstatic, divine union :

I abandoned and forgot myself,
Laying my face on my Beloved;
All things ceased; I went out from myself,
Leaving my cares
Forgotten among the lilies.[2]

Richard of St. Victor talks about this same ecstatic loss of individuality in the love of God :

> The mind of man is abstracted from itself by excess of joy and exultation, when its inmost self, drunk with the abundance of interior sweetness, forgets altogether what it is and what it will be . . . and in this condition of wonderful happiness, is suddenly transformed into a heavenly state.[3]

In addition to portraying blissful unity in terms of love, many of these same mystics invoke explicitly erotic imagery to convey a sense of the complete surrender to God required for mystical union. For example, St. John beseeches God to life him into a state of divine love :

Oh flame of love so living,
How tenderly you force
To my soul's innermost core your fiery probe !

---

1. Roy Campbell, Trans., *St. John of the Cross, Poems*, p. 45.

2. K. Kavanaugh, O. Rodriguez, Trans., *The Collected Works of St. John of the Cross*, p. 712.

3. Richard of Saint-Victor, *Selected Writings on Contemplation* (London : Faber and Faber, 1957) p. 189, quoted in R. C. Zaehner, *Concordant Discord*, p. 318.

Since now you've no misgiving,
End it, pursue your course
And for our sweet encounter tear the robe ![1]

Using the image of rapture, even Meister Eckhart, whose fundamental position is most frequently expressed in non-dualistic terms, moves towards theism when he adds that God "makes the enraptured soul to flee out of herself, for she is no more satisfied with anything that can be named. The spring of Divine Love . . . draws her out of herself."[2] St. Francois de Sales makes the same point when he says that "the ravished soul flows out in the wake of God's power of attraction."[3] Moreover, these same themes of erotic love and rapture are used to describe ecstatic, unifying experiences by Sufis and Hindu theists as well.[4]

For the Medieval Christians to whom we have referred, however, non-differentiated identification with God in ecstatic love was not the highest realization. Rather, this ecstasy was a passing experience which led to a permanent sense of union with God and a transformation of the soul only after ecstasy itself was lost in the period of desolation known as the "Dark Night." And in marked contrast with the highest realization in Advaita, the permanent union, or "Spiritual Marriage" between the soul and God in Christianity is characterized by a self-awareness which obeys, expresses and, indeed, becomes the will of God in worldly activity and service.[5] We will return to this point when we discuss the fourth level of consciousness and freedom.

What, then, is the significance of using love as the analogy for harmonious and blissful experience ? The answer becomes clear when we reflect for a moment on just what love symbolizes. For one thing, love implies the relationship and union of two separate entities. Specifically, in theistic traditions love is used to refer

1. *St. John of the Cross, Poems, op. cit.*, p. 45.

2. Meister Eckhart, "On the Steps of the Soul", quoted in Evelyn Underhill, *Mysticism*, p. 370. Rudolf Otto insists, however, that there is no "mysticism of exaggerated emotion" in Eckhart's love. Cf. *Mysticism East and West*. pp. 212-213.

3. St. Francois de Sales, *Traite de l'amour de Dieu*, 7.4., quoted in Zaehner, *C.D.*, p. 162.

4. Cf. Zaehner, *Hindu and Muslim Mysticism*, entire book.

5. Cf. Otto, *op. cit.*, p. 126; Zaehner, C. D., *op. cit.*, pp. 211, 321; Sidney Spencer, *Mysticism in World Religion*, pp. 253-257 for discussions of this point.

to the fact that the soul and the Lord, who are two, become one. Since this oneness can be attained only when the individual loses itself in the beloved, the second thing that love implies is an activity or process which ends with complete surrender. In the theistic context, this is expressed in terms of the surrender of the soul to God. And while this activity may begin as playful seduction, it quite frequently involves a great deal of effort and struggle on the part of the individual. The soul, in struggling to overcome its own resistance, asks the Lord to take it, to impose His will and thereby bring about the abandonment of individuality.

In Advaita, however, there is no duality. Rather, the Self is, ultimately, no other than undifferentiated reality. It thus makes no sense to talk in terms of love or any other kind of relationship between the Self and reality. Furthermore, it makes even less sense to talk, in the Advaitic context, of trying to lose the Self since the Self is, as we have seen, naturally autonomous, authentic and self-sufficient. The goal, then, is not to lose one's Self in identification with another but to stop the very process, called ignorance, by which one seems to lose oneself. For the Advaitin, whatever (sacred or profane) well-being, harmony or bliss one might experience derives ultimately from one's Self. Thus, when selecting an analogy for the experience of bliss, the Advaitin rejects love, which entails a struggle to overcome the separation between two beings and chooses dreamless sleep instead. The Advaitin sees three reasons for the superiority of this choice. First, deep sleep is a natural condition which involves neither struggle nor attainment. Second, the bliss of sleep consists in the negation of, rather than union with, the other. Third, sleep is a state of rest, a state in which both desire and activity are suspended. For these reasons sleep points to the richness, i.e., to the value, freedom and reality, which lies within the individual. And this, of course, is the whole point behind the interioristic hierarchy presented in the *Māṇḍūkya Upaniṣad.* For the Advaitin, then, deep sleep represents the greatest degree of unification of the subject possible in phenomenal experience. For this reason the third state of consciousness serves the Advaitin as the ideal analogy for harmonious and blissful spiritual experience.

Transcendental Consciousness

The final level of consciousness distinguished by Advaitins

is called, appropriately enough, the Fourth (*turīya*). Radically distinct in nature from the previous three states, *turīya* is the realization of absolute consciousness, representing the culmination of the interioristic hierarchy and embodying the fulfillment of the hierarchical criteria. As such, *turīya* is non-dual, non-sublatable, autonomous and certain awareness. It is freedom or liberation (*mokṣa*), the spiritual goal to which the Advaitic system points. *Turīya* is the transcendence of phenomenal experience, the annihilation of the limiting conditions which give birth to human bondage. *Turīya* is not an activity but is the eternal and all-pervading ground from which activity appears to emerge. *Turīya* is neither an object of knowledge nor a knowing subject but is transcendental, undifferentiated knowledge. Distinguishing it from the lower three levels, the *Māṇḍūkya Upaniṣad* reports :

> *Turīya* is not that which is conscious of the internal world, nor that which is conscious of the external world, nor that which is conscious of both, nor that which is a sentient mass, nor that which is simple consciousness, nor that which is insentient. (It is) unseen, not related to anything, incomprehensible, uninferable, unthinkable, indescribable, essentially of the nature of Consciousness constituting the Self alone, negation of all phenomena, the Peaceful, all Bliss and the Non-dual. This is the Ātman and it has to be realized.[1]

Let us study this Advaitic doctrine of salvation in more detail. As a non-dual realization, *turīya* transcends the conditions of space, time and causality. Going beyond spatial limitations, Ātman no longer identifies itself with either a body or with the appropriation of possessions or power. By transcending time, the Self is no longer concerned with change and with death. And by destroying the karmic, causal order, consciousness has removed itself from the influence of activity, i.e., the Self has been freed from its identification with agency and enjoyership as well as from the conditioning force of individual conduct. Says Śaṅkara, "mokṣa is not dependent like the fruits of actions on the conditions of space, time and cause; it is, in other words, neither short lived nor mediate in nature."[2] *Turīya* thus

1. *Māṇḍūkya Up.* 1.7.
2. *B.S.S.B.* 4.1.13.

represents a realization of what we might call impersonal immortality, an undifferentiated, eternal awareness transcending the moral responsibility by which the individual is determined and the transmigratory existence to which he is bound.

Turīya is a non-sublatable realization in the sense that liberation entails an eternally unchanging awareness which not only cancels all distinctions but eradicates their source, *avidyā*, as well. *Turīya* stands opposed to the process of sublation to the extent that the latter requires both an erroneous judgment and a re-evaluation of that judgment in the light of some new experience. As a non-sublatable realization, then, forever beyond the causal order and the duality between subject and obect, knowledge of Brahman is both irreversible, i.e., eternally pure, and undeniable, i.e., self-validating. Śaṅkara points to the radical distinction between Brahman and empirical knowledge by referring to the paradoxical Upaniṣadic remark that liberation "is not known by those who say they know it, but . . . is known by those who say that they do not know it."[1] Hyperbolic modesty aside, the point is that one for whom the distinction between the knower and the known still holds has failed to realize the uniquely non-dual, and therefore uniquely non-sublatable, nature of Brahman knowledge. That is, Brahman knowledge cannot be contradicted precisely because higher knowledge is eternally undifferentiated, while empirical knowledge, based upon the dualistic nature of phenomenal experience and logical thought, is the embodiment of opposition, discontinuity and contradiction. In other words, *mokṣa* is a state of eternal rest, equilibrium and continuity as opposed to the struggle, imbalance and contradictory nature of *saṁsāra*.

Advaitins place a great deal of importance on the claim that *turīya* is an autonomous realization because this point further confirms their distinction between the causal order and the means to freedom on the one hand and Brahman knowledge on the other. This claim is frequently made in the traditional literature by emphasizing that knowledge of Self is neither the result nor the product of an activity. The *Bṛhadāraṇyaka Upaniṣad*, for example, refers to the Self as "birthless," meaning that it is neither produced nor destroyed.[2] In his commentary on

1. *B.S.S.B.* 1.1.4., quoting *Kena Up.* 2.3.
2. *Bṛhad. Up. S.B.* 4.4.20, 4.4.22.

another section of the same text, Śaṅkara elaborates this point in detail :

> Liberation is not an effect — it is but the destruction of bondage, not a created thing. ... Production, attainment, modification and purification are the functions of [ritualistic and meditative] work. In other words, work can produce, or bring within reach, or modify, or purify something; it has not other functions besides these. ... And liberation is not one of these; we have already seen that it is simply hidden by ignorance.[1]

Thus *mokṣa* can neither be produced nor attained because, like the sun behind the clouds, it is already present. In this sense, liberation is the natural condition of consciousness, while the activity which appears to bring this realization about actually fails to effect consciousness at all. Quoting Śaṅkara once again :

> Though Ātman is an ever present reality, yet because of ignorance It is unrealized. On the destruction of ignorance, Ātman is realized. It is like the case of [searching for] the ornament on one's neck.[2]

Finally, *turīya* represents a realization of unqualified certainty and authentic fulfillment. As eternal rest or repose Brahman knowledge "gives one the conviction that one is completely blessed, and it requires no other witness than the testimony of one's own experience."[3] Being eternal, *mokṣa* is indestructible, and because it is fearless, "He who knows it as such becomes the fearless Brahman."[4] Since *turīya* is undifferentiated, "He who attains the Supreme Goal discards all such objects as name and form, and dwells as the embodiment of Infinite Consciousness and Bliss."[5] Further, as the ultimate source of value, *mokṣa* eradicates desire and the activity which desire motivates: "nothing remains to be desired or done by the man who really knows that the Ātman is one, permanent, and pure."[6] Once again,

1. *Bṛhad. Up. S.B.* 3.3.i.
2. Śaṅkara, *Ātmabodha*, 44.
3. *Bṛhad Up. S.B.* 4.4.9.
4. *Bṛhad. Up. S.B.* 4.4.25.
5. *Ātmabodha*, 40.
6. *S.S.B.* 4.3.14.

then, we see a sharp contrast drawn between all activity and the non-dual, non-sublatable, autonomous certainty of Brahman knowledge. This opposition parallels Śaṅkara's distinction, discussed above, between Brahman with (*saguṇa*) and without (*nirguṇa*) attributes, as well as the later Advaitic distinction between the two types of *samādhi*, determinate (*savikalpa*) and indeterminate (*nirvikalpa*). As this opposition between the path to liberation and the actual realization itself is one of the most prominent features of the Advaitic conception of liberation, it merits further elaboration.

Śaṅkara includes in his conception of phenomenal activity all secular and religious conduct. In addition, however, he treats the stages of the path (*jñāna-yoga*) to knowledge of Brahman as phenomenal activity as well.[1] That is, the cultivation of detachment from phenomenal objects through the process of discrimination is itself an activity grounded in ignorance, involving a subject who strives to attain a goal still beyond his grasp. The last and highest stage of this path, which culminates in the direct, non-dual intuition of Brahman, is called in different contexts concentration, contemplation and meditation (*dhāraṇā*, *dhyāna*, and *nididhyāsana* or *samādhi*). Dharmarāja argues that this highest stage is:

> That mental operation, which, in the case of the mind (*citta*) attracted to (external) objects by beginningless evil associations, is helpful to turn it away from (external) objects and secure firmness (for it) in respect to the self (alone) as object.[2]

Clearly, then, this last stage of the process of detachment from objects requires an object upon which to focus and, for those so inclined, to worship. In this context Śaṅkara interprets the various Upaniṣadic discussions of the manifestations of Brahman not as expressions of a pantheistic vision of reality, as some of his and our own contemporaries have maintained, but as objects of meditation.[3]

---

1. Cf. discussion of *jñāna-yoga* in Chapter I, above.
2. *Vedāntaparibhāṣā* 9.24-25.
3. Cf. Zaehner, *Hindu and Muslim Mysticism*, *op. cit.*, Chapter II., for example.

> The attribution of parts to Brahman is made with reference to its effects or modifications so that men of mediocre intelligence who are unable to fix their mind on nirguṇa Brahman, may be able to do so on some aspect of saguṇa Brahman for the purpose of devotion.[1]

In other words, "Brahman assumes two forms, one without limitations as the object of knowledge, and the other with limitations as the object of devotion. ... The latter however is the result of avidyā."[2]

Having drawn this radical distinction between action, the meditative path and the symbolic expressions or limited conceptions of Brahman on the one hand, and the non-dual knowledge of Brahman or absolute consciousness on the other, it is no surprise that Śaṅkara and his followers deny that the blissful experience of unity (*savikalpa samādhi, bhakti*), resulting from one-pointed concentration on the Lord, is the highest spiritual experience. Rather, they argue that true liberation refers to the unqualified transcendence of duality and to the absolute identification of the Self with Brahman which occurs in indeterminate spiritual experience (*nirvikalpa samādhi*) alone. K. C. Bhattacharyya has tried to express this difference between the highest meditative experience and true liberation by arguing that the former is accompanied by the realization of the illusory nature of duality through union with God, while the latter is accompanied by the complete transcendence of that realization itself.[3] In other words, determinate spiritual experience is a "duality in unity,"[4] while indeterminate spiritual experience transcends both duality and unity, or illusion and its harmonization in the Lord.

What, then, are the implications of this indeterminate spiritual experience for individual and social interaction in this world ? Clearly, liberation signals the release of the Self from the beginningless chain of *karma* and the cycle of transmigration. Thus *turīya*, as undifferentiated, eternal rest, must not only transcend the human realm (*lokavyavahāra*) of existence but also the higher

1. *B.S.S.B.* 3.2.33.
2. *B.S.S.B.* 1.1.12.
3. Bhattacharyya, *op. cit.*, pp. 28-29.
4. Deutsch, *op. cit.*, p. 13.

realms of Vedic cosmology, such as heaven (*svarga*) and the god-realms (*deva-loka*) as well, since habitation in these realms is also determined by the law of *karma*. This would seem to imply, therefore, that true liberation can only take place upon the physical death of one who has realized Brahman. This doctrine, called *videha mukti*, does indeed receive support in Advaitic literature. For example, Śaṅkara says that :

> If both good and evil deeds are said not to cling to the person who has realized Brahman, or are said to be destroyed in their effects so far as he is concerned, it follows that he attains to mokṣa as soon as his body falls.[1]

Again, "when the serene being, after having risen from the body, meets the highest light, it manifests in its own form."[2] And if this were the only type of liberation allowed by the Advaitins, we would have to conclude that, because the *videha mukti* never lives in the world, *mokṣa* makes neither a positive nor a negative contribution to samsāric interaction.

There is another understanding of liberation presented in the Upaniṣads and their Advaitic commentaries, however, which shows the preceding conclusion to be one-sided. This second doctrine is called liberation in life (*jīvanmukti*) and refers to one who remains alive in a body while actually realizing that he is a disembodied and immortal Self. The *Bṛhadāraṇyaka Upaniṣad* tries to illustrate the de-identification and non-relationship between the Self and the *jīvanmukta*'s body by likening the latter to a lifeless slough, cast off and no longer connected to a snake.[3] In more technical terms, Śaṅkara explains the continued existence of the body after liberation by distinguishing three types of *karma*. The first two types, *sañcita* and *kriyamāṇa*, refer to action done in the past which has not yet borne fruit and action done in the present which is to bear fruit, respectively. These two types of *karma*, Śaṅkara says, are completely destroyed by Brahman knowledge.[4] The third type is called *prārabdha* and refers to action done in the past which has already begun to bear

1. *B.S.S.B.* 4.1.15.
2. *B.S.S.B.* 4.4.1., quoting *Chānd. Up*. 8.12.3.
3. *Bṛhad. Up. S.B.* 4.4.7; *B.S.S.B.* 1.1.4.
4. *B.S.S.B.* 3.3.32.; 4.1.15.

fruit through the formation and vitalization of the present body itself. And this type of *karma,* Śaṅkara argues, cannot be stopped until death, "just as an arrow which leaves the bow continues to move so long as its initial motion is not exhausted."[1] But the fact remains that while the *prārabdha karma* continues to motivate bodily activity, the *jīvanmukta* remains completely detached from, and unaffected by, it.

But what sort of life does a *jīvanmukta* lead in the world ? Clearly, he experiences the eternal tranquility characteristic of *turīya*.

> Relinquishing attachment to illusory external happiness, the Self-abiding jīvanmukta, satisfied with the Bliss derived from Ātman, shines inwardly, like a lamp placed inside a jar.[2]

And how does he act towards the world ? Since the *jīvanmukta* is completely detached from activity and its results, he is free from both the consequences of, and judgments concerning, good and evil. In this sense he is thoroughly amoral, and although he would not be karmically affected by committing murder, for example, such an act, being motivated by egoism, is totally alien to his nature.[3] Along with the *jīvanmukta*'s detachment and amorality comes the realization of the identity of "others" with "his" Self.

> The yogi endowed with complete enlightenment sees, through the eye of Knowledge, the entire universe in his own Self and regards everything as the Self and nothing else.[4]

> Thus, the *jīvanmukta* voluntarily relates to illusory forms, but The fact that he now comes to think cosmically signifies that he will feel equally attached to all that is, and that whatever he does will be inspired by love which knows neither preferences nor exclusions.[5]

---

1. *B.S.S.B.* 3.2.32; *Bṛhad. Up. S.B.* 1.4.10. Another favorite analogy for *prārabdha karma* is the potter's wheel, which continues to rotate for some time after initially being propelled.
2. *Ātmabodha*, 51.
3. Cf. *Kausītakī Up*. 3.1., where a series of heinous crimes which fail to affect the *Jīvanmukta* are listed.
4. *Ātmabodha*, 47.
5. M. Hiriyanna, *Popular Essays in Indian Philosophy*, p. 22. It becomes clear from descriptions of the radiation of being manifested by a *jīvanmukta* that the love and harmony characteristic of *savikalpa samādhi* and *saguṇa Brahman* are complementary rather than opposed to the unqualified non-duality of the highest realization, *nirvikalpa samādhi*. Cf. Deutsch, *op. cit.*, pp. 12-14.

In other words, the *jīvanmukta* relates to all beings with a universal radiation of light emerging from the realization that beings are none other than pure consciousness or Self. Furthermore, this universal love is freely expressed; the *jīvanmukta* is neither motivated by any injunction or obligation to duty, nor is he under the direction of, or service to, a Divine will.[1] In this sense, the Advaitic contention that love is extended to an object on the basis of the pleasure love provides for the lover himself, which seems to replace true compassion for others with a resignation to human selfishness, is hereby transformed in the being of the *jīvanmukta* into an expression of all-encompassing, non-exclusive love. And while Śaṅkara indicates that the wise man lives a simple, unconceited and quiet life,[2] he nevertheless enjoins a man who recognizes that he is bound to the world to seek out one of these liberated beings.

> He must necessarily approach a *guru* who is characterised by composure of mind, self-control, love, etc. Even one that is well-versed in the *śāstras* should not set about seeking Brahma-knowledge by himself.[3]

Thus, the *jīvanmukta* is a remover of darkness (*guru*), a beacon light of the universe.[4] He has realized the eternal bliss for which devout Hindus supplicate daily :

> From non-Being lead me to Being.
> From darkness lead me to light.
> From death lead me to immortality.[5]

The Advaitic doctrine of liberation is obviously quite different from the conception of freedom which has been upheld by most Western philosophers since Hobbes. For Hobbes, freedom or human liberty consists in the absence of any external restraint preventing one from acting according to one's desires. By conceiving of freedom in these terms, Hobbes was trying to resolve certain philosophical problems, such as the opposition

1. *B.S.S.B.* 4.4.9.
2. *B.S.S.B.* 3.4.50.
3. *Muṇḍaka Up. S.B.* 1,2.12.
4. Bhattacharyya, *op. cit.*, p. 59.
5. *asato mā sadgamaya, tamaso mā jyotirgamaya, mṛtyor māmṛtam gamaya. Bṛhad. Up.* 1.3.28.

between freedom and determinism and the relationship between Divine omniscience, determinism and moral responsibility, which were matters of concern for Western thinkers from Hellenic and Hellenistic times. Hobbes's conception of liberty as freedom from restraint was echoed by Locke who, while rejecting his predecessor's materialism, defined freedom as "being able to act or not to act, according as we shall choose or will."[1] One measure of the influence of this position is that it lies at the heart of the American Declaration of Independence and Western liberalism in general.

Clearly, to the extent that "freedom from" points to a doctrine of self-determination, it moves in a direction which is not incompatible with the Advaitic conception of freedom. But the difference between the two lies in the fact that the Advaitic conception of Self-determination goes far beyond the absence of external restraint and the freedom to pursue pleasant or creative individual preservation. Advaitic Self-determination requires the absence of all desire, choice and will. It means impersonal, immortal perfection, beyond activity and all finite determination which, in the Advaitic context, are equivalent to limitation. In other words, the Advaitin's Self-determination precludes finitude and transcends what we conventionally call self-determination itself.

We have already mentioned certain similarities between the Advaitic description of *savikalpa samādhi* and Medieval Christian mystical descriptions of ecstasy. When we turn to the question of the comparison between Advaitic liberation and the salvation of the Christian mystic, however, we meet with more differences than similarities. For one thing, to the extent that these Christians attempted to remain orthodox, they were unable to claim an experience of final salvation in this world, such as we find in the Advaitic theory of *jīvanmukti*. According to Christian dogma, no amount of perfection or blessedness attained in this world can approach God's infinite perfection and thus true salvation, or eternal life in heaven, can only be attained after physical death. This is no less true for Meister Eckhart, whose vision of God is at times expressed in pantheistic and even monistic terms, and for Dionysius the Areopagite, whose

1. John Locke, *Two Treatises of Government*, II.ii.4.

negative theological description of mystical experience is similar to the *via negativa* found in Advaita, than it is for more straightforward theists such as St. Teresa and St. John of the Cross.

This point of Christian dogma aside, there is another and equally important distinction to be established. That is, the Medieval mystics uniformly expressed their highest realization, the divinization of the individual soul in the Spiritual Marriage with God, in terms of an active life of service and work in accordance with Divine will. In addition to the fact that this Spiritual Marriage involves the transformation rather than the transcendence of the individual soul found in Advaita, the Spiritual Marriage also entails the subjugation or even the destruction of individual self-will and its replacement with "obedience to God in deed and life."[1] Otto says that in Eckhart's highest experience, the will :

> Becomes none other than the very will of God, who wills and works, lives and creates through our will, so that there is but one will, which is likewise essential justice.[2]

The Spiritual Marriage is thus a condition in which the soul, through action, service and duty, becomes the vehicle for the expression of the just, good and in all other ways perfect will of God. In contrast, we have seen that the *jīvanmukta*, who is said to have transcended divine as well as individual will, radiates the love of the fullness of being universally but does not get involved in any of the mundane work and service which characterize the lives of many Medieval Christian mystics. On the other hand, the *jīvanmukta* is not inactive, but he waits for students to approach and then directs his attention primarily to helping them realize the illusory nature of all name and form. While it would seem to be impossible to evaluate and compare the actual experiences of freedom portrayed through these different descriptions of liberated life, it is interesting to note their difference in both expression and emphasis and to wonder to what extent this diversity reflects a cultural rather than a spiritual difference, if indeed, such a distinction can be meaningfully drawn at all.

Another Western source suggesting important similarities and differences with the Advaitic conception of liberation is the

1. Otto, *op. cit.*, p. 126.
2. *Ibid.*, p. 126.

doctrine of impersonal immortality of the Latin Averroists. The foremost of these thinkers, Siger de Brabant, followed Averroes' monopsychistic interpretation of Aristotle's doctrine of the active intellect and claimed that all men share in the same rational soul. For Siger, man's highest realization, the beautific vision of God, was nothing more nor less than man's union with the one rational soul. To the extent that Siger was faithful to Aristotle's active intellect, furthermore, it can be inferred that he was philosophically opposed to the Christian doctrine that God created, and could destroy, the human soul. Thus, Siger's impersonal soul was not only immortal but eternal or beginningless as well. On this latter point the Latin Averroists clearly seem to be approaching the Advaitic conception of liberation. But a major difference between the two consists in the fact that Siger's immortal soul is rational, while the Advaitin specifies that Brahman knowledge is both supra-rational and supra-intellectual. The Advaitin wants to indicate by these terms that absolute consciousness is beyond the dualistic nature of rationality and that the highest knowledge cannot be comprehended through intellectual activity.

> In the deepest sense of the highest truth is that which Vedāntins call the inexhaustible, beyond Being as beyond non-being. It is reality alone, nothing else.[1]

There is, however, one doctrine of freedom in the West which is identical with the Advaitin's *turīya* on almost all important points, at least according to the analysis of Neoplatonism offered by Professor Staal. Staal claims that freedom for both Plotinus and the Advaitin means "to transcend the level of human freedom and to go beyond to the divine perfection, where choice of an evil possibility is no longer realizable."[2]

1. *Bhagavad Gītā S.B.* 11.37.

2. Staal, *op. cit.*, p. 229. Staal makes the point that the *jīvanmukta* "acts in accordance with the good, automatically and freely" and does not possess the human freedom to choose between good and evil, which is a "freedom" possessed by a soul in bondage. Deutsch contends that the *jīvanmukta* can logically perform any act he wishes, although psychologically he is incapable of performing an evil, i.e., egoistic, act. Deutsch, *op. cit.*, p. 102. The latter position seems to be closer to the spirit of Advaitic thought since the Advaitin argues that the liberated man transcends, through non-attachment to the fruits of action, the duality between good and evil.

There is undoubtedly much validity to the similarity that Staal points out, although he passes over perhaps a bit too briefly some of the significant differences between the two. For one thing, as Staal notes, Plotinus failed to accept that one could attain the highest degree of freedom while alive in the world. This hesitation must have been grounded at least partially in the fact that Plotinus felt he had only attained a glimpse of the highest truth during his four distinct ecstatic experiences. On the other hand, we must note that the Advaitic analysis seems inadequate to explain just how the *jīvanmukta* successfully negotiates his mundane life activity because, in some very basic sense, the liberated man has actually transcended the activity characteristic of modified consciousness itself. For another thing, as Staal fails to point out, Plotinus' divine perfection, which precludes an evil choice, is based on the realization of the old Platonic Form of the Good and thus represents a variety of rational or intellectual ethics, i.e., that one cannot knowingly do wrong or evil. On the other hand, in the strictest sense, the Advaitin cannot knowingly do anything, and he certainly fails to identify with any activity performed by the body either as his own or in terms of good and evil. Once again, then, we see that the Advaitin's liberation is supra-rational, beyond the metaphysical good and evil which seem to underlie Plotinus' conception of freedom. Thus, Śaṅkara ends his *Ātmabodha* with the following :

> He who, renouncing all activities, worships in the sacred and stainless shrine of Ātman, which is independent of time, place, and distance; which is present everywhere; which is the destroyer of heat and cold, and the other opposites; and which is the giver of eternal happiness, becomes all-knowing and all-pervading and attains Immortality.

1. *Ātmabodha*, 68.

CHAPTER V

CONCLUSION : A CRITICAL EVALUATION OF THE ADVAITIC TREATMENT OF CONSCIOUSNESS

This chapter subjects the Advaitic theory of consciousness to critical evaluation by focusing attention on a number of problems that arise in conjunction with the most central and distinctive feature of the theory, i.e., the radical ontological discontinuity between absolute and modified consciousness.

To review, we have seen that the two orders of consciousness refer simultaneously to distinct levels of reality, knowledge and value. Thus, absolute consciousness is unchanging and non-dual reality, eternally self-luminous awareness and the blissful transcendence of all finitude and limitation. Modified consciousness, on the other hand, represents the concealment and distortion of reality which is the changing world of appearance, awareness based upon the illusory separation of subject and object, and bondage to inherently unfulfilling life activity. In this sense, these two distinct levels point to radically opposed kinds of experience, i.e., while man appears to be the victim of misfortune and misery, he is in reality both unaffected by circumstances and eternally free. Furthermore, while phenomenal experience is illusory, it nevertheless represents the means by which modified consciousness is cancelled and liberation realized. The Advaitic theory of consciousness thus stands as a statement of hope, as an injunction to live a just and virtuous life, to pursue higher knowledge and to transcend the delusion of suffering.

One problem, which arises from the claim that the realization of pure consciousness is an experience of radical discontinuity, consists in the fact that there seem to be two possible candidates for this realization; determinate and indeterminate spiritual experience. That is, the discontinuity must either be experienced along with the realization of the unification, or the transcendence, of all distinctions. If the Advaitin tries to argue, on the one hand, that determinate spiritual experience represents an awareness radically distinct from phenomenal consciousness, then one wonders how the *yogin* at this level enjoys the harmonious experience of duality in unity. Ought not duality be transcended altogether in the realization of the truth of a system whose very name (*advaita*) indicates a reality independent of, rather than complementary to, multiplicity ? To the extent that the Advaitin does indeed wish to claim that determinate spiritual experience is an awareness radically distinct from the conditions of ignorance and bondage, however, he comes close to the pantheism to which, as we have previously seen, he is opposed. On the other hand, there is at least one good reason why the Advaitin does not wish to reserve the radical distinction between bondage and liberation for indeterminate spiritual experience. For to do so, and thereby follow the teaching of non-duality to its logical conclusion, would be to deny that the liberated man relates to the suffering mass of humanity at all and would deprive him of his role as the illuminating light of mankind.

We can comment upon, rather than resolve, this ambiguity by noting that it seems to represent an inevitable dilemma facing any transcendental system of thought, i.e., at some point a transition between the phenomenal and transcendental orders must be accounted for in terms of some entity or faculty which can bridge the gap between the opposing orders.[1] The problem is made all the more acute for the Advaitin because he alone denies any positive basis for continuity, either in terms of rational knowledge, emotional surrender, or volitional activity, between the lower and higher levels of awareness. Thus, while we are not surprised to find the Advaitin's determinate spiritual experience, i.e., harmonious unity in the Lord, straddling the fence between duality and non-duality, the introduction of just such a transitional state, relating modified and absolute consciousness, seems to reflect that there is something philosophically dissatisfying with the notion of a radical break in experience. The Advaitin, for his part, responds that this radical discontinuity is only a problem for one who assumes that the human

1. As an initial amplification of this claim, it can be argued that Plato's Forms represent a transition between the Form of the Good and phenomenal particulars, that Plotinus' second hypostasis (*nous*) serves as a transition between the One and individuality, that Spinoza's account of the human mind makes possible the movement from finitude to eternity, and that the Mahāyāna Buddhist's ideal of compassion is the bridge between *saṃsāra* and *nirvāṇa*.

mind should be the final arbiter of reality. And just such an assumption, of course, has characterized the mainstream of Western philosophical thinking, at least since the time of Parmenides. In other words, we in the West have long believed, and acted as if, we were rational animals capable of using intellect to unravel the mysteries of the universe and the meaning of life. In this milieu, the Advaitin's claim of an ontological distinction between reason and reality must initially seem somewhat mind-boggling and, if taken seriously, demands a re-evaluation of the scope, limits and purpose not only of philosophy but of human life itself.

Moving beyond this point, we find that the hierarchical vision, a central component in the Advaitic theory of consciousness, follows directly from the experience of radical discontinuity between the two levels of consciousness. That is, implicit in the Advaitic distinction between two levels is the claim that one is immeasurably or qualitatively superior to the other. As we have seen, this discontinuity provides the Advaitin with the crieria in terms of which he tries to order the variety of human experience. On the one hand, we have the realization of Brahman, an eternally non-contradicted, autonomous and authentic experience. On the other hand, we have phenomenal experience or modified consciousness ranked, from the perspective of either the subject or object, according to the degree to which it reflects the criteria characteristic of Brahman realization.

A number of problems arise both from the Advaitin's attempt to characterize the highest experience and from his attempt to establish a hierarchical distinction between phenomenal and absolute consciousness in terms of these characteristics. One such problem involves the attempt to relate two radically distinct levels hierarchically. If the two levels are qualitatively discontinuous, i.e., share no common characteristics, then how can a criterion derived from a characteristic of one level be applied to the other? In other words, how can phenomenal experience be less authentic, for example, than Brahman realization? Ought not phenomenal experience be referred to in terms of inauthenticity itself, just as we say that phenomenal experience is sublatable in contrast to the non-sublatability of Brahman realization? Of course, the answer is in the affirmative. But doesn't this admission undermine the very basis for establishing a hierarchical relationship between the two orders and leave one with an opposition or duality between the two instead ? While the Advaitin does acknowledge that a certain opposition characterizes the two hierarchical levels, we have seen that he denies that this opposition contradicts the ultimate non-duality of Brahman by contrasting the concept of difference with that of distinction. To be different, two entities must be equally real, while to be distinct, one entity or level must, by the Advaitin's definition, be in hierarchical, sublatable relationship to the other. The implication behind this definition is that the hierarchical relationship between the two levels obtains only from the lower standpoint of unenlightened experience : there is neither a hierarchy nor a relationship entailed by Brahman realization itself. In this way, then, the utter non-duality of the real is upheld.

Another, related problem which arises in the context of the Advaitin's hierarchical vision is not how the hierarchical criteria can be applied to two levels of reality, truth or consciousness, but just what the Advaitin means when he talks in terms of two levels. That is, the implication behind the claim that there are levels is that we can meaningfully ask : levels *of what* ? But when the Advaitin argues for the radical discontinuity between the lower and higher levels of consciousness, for example, we must begin to wonder whether the concept of consciousness can hold up under the strain of such usage. Can we meaningfully talk in terms of two levels of consciousness, two levels of reality, or two levels of truth ? The Advaitin insists that we can indeed talk in these terms, although his two justifications for this use of language reflect a certain ambivalence on his part. The first justification is based on the claim that absolute consciousness is as real, intelligent and blissful as *śruti* asserts. The lower level of modified consciousness, from this perspective, is certainly not real, but neither is it unreal. Rather, modified consciousness is indescribable in terms of either reality or unreality (*sadasadanirvacanīya*), which is to say that it is at once ultimately illusory, or false, and yet not self-contradictory. In this sense the Advaitin, as we have previously argued, makes a concession to the efficacy of phenomena when he treats this world as the lower level of consciousness, reality or truth.

On the other hand, the Advaitin is quite clear that many of

these problems concerning the characterization of the highest experience and the hierarchical criteria derive from his own fundamental principle that every determination is a limitation and a negation. Since absolute "consciousness" is unlimited and beyond contradiction, it cannot be adequately characterized. In fact, we have seen that the Advaitin argues that there is a basic incompatibility between conceptualization and the realization of Brahman that is best indicated by the Upaniṣadic *neti, neti*. The Advaitin's second justification for talking in terms of levels of reality and consciousness, offered from this perspective, is that although all concepts, including reality and consciousness, are ultimately illusory, the realm of phenomenal experience, including conventional and philosophical linguistic usage, has a practical efficacy that warrants this concession to ignorance in the form of speech. Just as a dream assailant can prompt us to awaken, so, the Advaitin argues, illusory experience provides the means by which to transcend itself. The concession in this case does not consist in the willingness to refer to the lower level in terms of concepts which, strictly speaking, apply only to the higher level. Rather, the concession consists in the willingness to conceptualize at all. Thus, the ambivalence between these two justifications, i.e., between saying that the world is *sadasadanirvacanīya* and that Brahman is *neti, neti,* lies precisely in the dilemma of trying to provide an account of human experience while recognizing (or maintaining) at the same time that reality is beyond the limits of our ability to provide just such an account. In other words, the Advaitin claims a certainty and indubitability for his non-dual spiritual experience which remains radically distinct from, and unaffected by, the relative success of his attempt to categorize that realization and its relationship to all other human experience. The Advaitin's transcendental commitment, however, does not lead to anti-intellectualism on his part. Rather, he articulates and defends his vision in spite of the problems and inconsistencies confronted and the "concessions" that he admits having to make in the course of trying, paradoxically enough, to speak the unspeakable to one who cannot, as yet, hear.

Along these same lines we have seen that whatever validity we attribute to the Advaitin's insistence upon the continuity of absolute consciousness in all experience, i.e., upon the persistence of the Ātman in modified consciousness, must finally be based on the cancellation of individual experience itself, just as the sun is seen to persist when the clouds covering it disperse. Since absolute consciousness is not actually transformed into phenomenal experience, the latter is merely an illusory appearance of Brahman and its relationship to Brahman also remains an illusion. How, then, can the Advaitin argue for the existence of absolute consciousness from the continuity or persistence of awareness in the three admittedly illusory phenomenal states? Clearly, he cannot. Even if the continuity of self-awareness in phenomenal experience is granted, in spite of the objections against claiming self-awareness during deep sleep and the evident contradiction involved in claiming it during "unconscious" states, we are merely acknowledging the continuity of apparent rather than absolute consciousness. Having established a radical distinction between reality and appearance, the one and the many, eternal rest and temporal change, the Advaitin's attempts to argue from the latter back to the former may be systematically instructive and spiritually edifying, but they cannot be logically conclusive.

Up to this point, our critical evaluation has focused on internal difficulties faced by the Advaitin as a result of his claim that there is a radical distinction between absolute and modified consciousness, between Brahman and the world. Let us now deal with what, it can be argued, is a serious omission or shortcoming in the Advaitic theory of consciousness following directly from this same radical discontinuity. We have seen that the radical distinction between modified and absolute consciousness is based on the cancellation or contradiction of the former through the realization of the latter, and that this experience of discontinuity provides the Advaitin with the basis for establishing his hierarchy of consciousness. Thus, the Advaitin's hierarchical vision is grounded in the principle that the transcendence of one level of experience by another involves the cancellation, i.e., the denial and elimination, of the transcended level. What is excluded from this vision, then, is the idea that consciousness develops, that some continuity between levels of experience allows the lower level to grow, evolve or contribute to the formation and existence of the higher level.

The Advaitin's fundamentally static conception of consciousness manifests in a number of different ways. First, the Advaitin contends that absolute consciousness is absolute or real precisely because it is unchanging. We have seen that Śaṅkara describes the realization of Brahman as eternal bliss, while change, modification and activity serve as synonyms for the lower level of consciousness. Second, the Advaitin discusses the various levels of modified consciousness in terms of states (*sthāna*), a noun derived from the verbal root *sthā,* meaning to remain, stand still or rest on something. Thus, even when he is talking about modified consciousness and grouping a variety of phenomenal experiences together in one of the three lower hierarchical levels, the Advaitin uses a word which implies a fixed, stable and distinct static state.

Of course, the Advaitin could incorporate some developmental account of the experience of the conditions of space, time and causality in waking consciousness along the lines of the Swiss psychologist Jean Piaget, for example, without violating his claim that these conditions represent the limitation imposed by ignorance on consciousness at this level.[1] All the Advaitin need do is argue that these conditions are actually latent subconscious patterns (*saṁskāra*) which require a certain period of experimental development before they can manifest and exert their influence as characteristics of the mature waking state. Similarly, since the Advaitin does not wish to claim that the discontinuity in terms of which the three lower levels of consciousness are distinguished is equivalent to the radical discontinuity distinguishing modified from absolute consciousness, he can certainly argue that there is some growth, development and mutual influence among the three states. For example, we have seen that the Advaitin admits the influence of waking experience upon dream and vice versa. Thus, moral and intellectual development achieved in waking consciousness can be reflected in a change in the quality of one's dream experience, and dream messages can prompt a desire for growth through a change in some aspect of one's waking experience. Further, certain

1. For a discussion of Piaget's developmental conception of space, time and causality, see : Jean Piaget, *The Child's Conception of Physical Causality*, trans. by M. Gabain; *The Child's Conception of Time*, trans. by A. J. Pomerans; *The Child's Conception of Space*, trans. by F. J. Langdon and J. L. Lunzer.

psychological changes can produce great emotional turmoil which make it extremely difficult even to "fall" into deep sleep, while blissful sleep experience itself might conceivably convince one of the possibility of experiencing eternal tranquility and encourage one to try to realize Brahman. In spite of this ability to incorporate a developmental model into his account of modified consciousness, however, the Advaitin remains unable to reconcile the notion of development with the level of absolute consciousness, i.e., with the fullness of being which is eternally perfect and complete.

We find a sharp contrast with the Advaitic position on this point in the thought of G. W. F. Hegel, who argues that the superiority of his philosophical system over all previous systems of thought consists precisely in his formulation of a developmental conception of absolute consciousness.[1] Absolute consciousness or Spirit (*Geist*) signifies for Hegel a teleological process of becoming, i.e., the actual manifestation of reality or Reason in and through the dynamic movement of both nature and history. In following the implications of this claim that infinite Spirit expresses itself in and through the finite, Hegel is committed, in his *Phenomenology of Spirit,* to try to trace the evolution of human consciousness as the self-manifestation of the development of reality itself. Without entering a discussion of the specific stages of the ascent of consciousness presented by Hegel is this text, let us outline the model in terms of which he explains Spirit's development.

For Hegel, the movement of Spirit is motivated by its own inner necessity and can be reduced to three moments : immediacy; alienation; and self-certainty. The first moment, Spirit in itself, signifies immediate, undifferentiated objectivity. In this moment, Spirit expresses itself as Nature, i.e., as unself-conscious, pre-reflective essence or substance.[2] While Hegel thus initiates the developmental model of Spirit with undifferentiated substance, or pure being, he nevertheless insists that this conception of reality is "abstract," i.e., limited and incomplete,

---

1. This claim is the underlying theme of the Preface to Hegel's *Phenomenology of Spirit,* trans. and ed. by Walter Kaufmann in *Hegel : Texts and Commentary.*

2. Jean Hyppolite, *Genesis and Structure of Hegel's Phenomenology of Spirit* trans. by Samuel Cherniak and John Heckman , p. 583.

precisely because it consists of Spirit as potentiality, prior to and lacking self-knowledge of its own actuality, i.e., of its implicit and necessary future development. In other words, he insists that objective substance "is more than itself; it is itself and its other"[1] and that it "lives" by moving itself to become something other than itself.[2]

Hegel tries to capture this living dimension of reality in his formulation of the second moment of Spirit, i.e., the self-conscious alienation of Spirit for itself, by arguing that substance is also subject.[3] For Hegel, a subject is that which mediates between a self and its development into something different. In this second moment, then, Spirit negates or contradicts itself as immediate being in itself and thereby becomes a mediate, experiencing subject, or an object other than and for itself. And precisely in terms of this claim that substance is subject Hegel feels he has overcome the relativism and subjectivism in which, he argues, the "epistemologists' from Descartes to Kant and Fichte had become hopelessly mired. That is, Hegel's self-conscious 'I' is no longer prevented, by the duality between the subject and object, from stepping beyond itself and actually knowing reality because a self-conscious subject is now defined as that which becomes the other in the negation of itself. Thus, the stages of nature and history and the levels of human consciousness are actually steps in Spirit's negation and development of itself as the for itself. But ordinary human consciousness is not aware that its self-conscious experience of the other, i.e., of itself as the other than itself, is actually consciousness of Spirit.

The third moment in Hegel's development of Spirit, resulting from the alienation and negation characteristic of the second moment, is just this self-conscious awareness that substance is subject. In other words, the end of the development of absolute consciousness in Hegel's system, called absolute knowledge or Philosophy, is the reconciliation of Spirit in itself with Spirit for itself and the revelation of Spirit as the in and for itself.[4]

1. Cf. Hyppolite, pp. 575-76, 578-79.
2. Kaufman, *op. cit.*, p. 28.
3. *Iibd.*, pp. 28-32.
4. *Ibid.*, p. 38.

And the rational self-certainty characteristic of this moment derives from the fact that consciousness, in absolute knowledge, can look into itself and find Reality precisely because the totality of human awareness and, therefore, the totality of thought, is identical with the awareness of the totality of Reality.[1] The individual who attains absolute knowledge thus becomes fully rational, self-determining and free. In this sense, Hegel's absolute knowledge is the activity by which Spirit "transcends itself as finite Spirit"[2] and becomes one with the infinite system of Reality.

But how does this developmental movement of Spirit actually take place ? According to Hegel, the movement from one level of consciousness to the next occurs through Spirit's inner necessity, i.e., its immanent entelechy. "From its beginning, naive consciousness aims at the entire content of knowledge in all its richness."[3] The problem with each finite level of experience, and the reason that consciousness can find no satisfactory resting place short of absolute knowledge, is that at each finite level "[w]hat consciousness takes to be true is revealed to be illusory; consciousness must abandon its first belief and move on to another."[4] In other words, at each finite level of experience consciousness discovers the unsatisfactoriness or negation inherent in it. While this dissatisfaction is accompanied by existential doubt and disquiet,[5] and is purely negative for the level of consciousness discovered to be inadequate, Hegel argues that doubt is also positive in the sense that it brings about the next higher level. Consciousness "incessantly transcends itself, and the death of what it held as its truth is the appearance of a new truth."[6] Thus, "negation is always *determinate* negation.... To be cognizant of one's error is to be cognizant of another truth : the perceived error implies a new truth."[7]

Explained in these terms, Hegel's account of the transcendence

1. Quenton Lauer, S. J ., *Hegel's Idea of Philosophy*, p. 3.
2. Hyppolite, *op. cit.*, p. 599.
3. *Ibid.*, p. 15.
4. *Ibid.*, p. 12.
5. *Ibid.*, p. 13.
6. *Ibid.*, p. 18.
7. *Ibid.*, p. 14.

of finitude through the process of negation (*Aufhebung*) seems quite close to the Advaitic conception of the process of cancellation (*bādha*). In fact, the similarities between the Hegelian and Advaitic conceptions of the experience of contradiction have prompted scholars to translate both *Aufhebung* and *bādha* as "sublation." But we have argued above that a developmental conception of absolute consciousness is a contradiction in terms for the Advaitin precisely because his absolute is eternally perfect and complete in itself and radically discontinuous from the lower level of consciousness. Thus the Advaitin intends a thoroughgoing elimination of phenomena when he talks about its sublation in Brahman knowledge. Hegel, on the other hand, uses the mechanism of sublation to guarantee the continuity between each level of consciousness and to justify his claim that Spirit does indeed develop, by insisting that *Aufhebung* "has a twofold meaning in language, in that it means to preserve, to *maintain,* and at the same time to make cease, *to put an end to.*"[1] For Hegel, then, the transcendence of each level of consciousness involves both overcoming the limitation entailed by that level and incorporating its partial truth into the knowledge of the next higher level. As the culmination of this developmental process, the absolute knowledge which finally emerges in history with Hegel's Spirit in and for itself includes detailed and systematic, i.e., rational, knowledge of all the stages that preceded it. Thus, Hegel's fully-developed consciousness unites all opposition, e.g., between finite and infinite, action and knowledge, by reconciling or harmonizing them in Reason, while unchanging, absolute consciousness in the Advaitic tradition entails not only the total elimination of all opposition but a realization which is eternally distinct from all activity, conceptualization and developments within phenomenal consciousness as well. Where Hegel's reality is fully rational, Śaṅkara distinguishes rationality from spirituality, which is to say that, for Śaṅkara, reality leaves reason far behind.

More direct evidence of the fundamental incompatibility between the Advaitic doctrine of radical discontinuity and a

1. G. W. F. Hegel, *The Science of Logic* I, 94, as quoted by Andries Sarlemijn, *Hegel's Dialectic,* p. 84. In order to emphasize this distinction between Hegel's *Aufhebung* and the Advaitic *bādha,* Professor Deutsch has translated the latter as subration. Deutsch, *op. cit.,* p. 15.

developmental model of consciousness can be seen quite clearly in the Integral philosophy of the Neo-Vedāntin, Sri Aurobindo. One of the primary features of Aurobindo's system is his sustained attempt to reconcile many cogent but often conflicting trends of Indian and Western thought. Perhaps the most central of all these integrations, and the one most relevant to our present discussion, is his synthesis of the traditional Advaitic conception of Brahman with the theory of evolution. According to Aurobindo, Brahman directly transforms itself, through a process of gradual descent called involution, into matter or the physical universe. Further, since the last grade or degree of descent is simultaneously the first stage of the ascent, matter is alive with the intention of Brahman to evolve through it.[1] For Aurobindo, then, Brahman, as the multidimensional fullness of being, is the unity of the formless and eternal with changing, evolving forms. In this sense, he argues for a realistic ontology with each finite individual and each historical, cultural and artistic development representing both a real determination of Brahman and a particular stage in its evolutionary ascent.

Throughout his writings, Aurobindo acknowledges his debt to various philosophical, psychological and scientific theories quite openly, although he also insists upon the superiority of his Integral philosophy to each of these component parts. For example, while commending the scientific theory of evolution for its accurate analysis of the outward and visible details "of Nature's execution, with the physical development of things in Matter and the law of development of life and mind in Matter,"[2] he objects that this explanation cannot adequately account for the complexity found in the human body and mind.[3] Arguing that such complexity can only be explained through the intervention of a supraphysical power, Aurobindo replaces the mechanical conception of physical, biological change found in science, which was the source of his own evolutionary inspiration, with a teleological account of the development of spiritually informed mind and matter.[4]

1. Sri Aurobindo, *The Life Divine*, I., pp. 325-26, *passim*.
2. Aurobindo, *op. cit.*, II., p. 662.
3. *Ibid.*, II., p. 667.
4. Sri Aurobindo, *The Supramental Manifestation*, p. 232, reprinted in *The Essential Aurobindo*, ed. Robert A. McDermott, p. 61. Aurobindo

Similarly, Aurobindo readily acknowledges his debt to Vedic thought, and especially to Advaita, although he is committed to exposing its shortcomings from his own point of view as well. Specifically, Aurobindo objects to the Advaitic conceptions of reality as unqualified, changeless Brahman, and of liberation as an eternally peaceful, static and undifferentiated realization. Instead, he maintains that evolution and timeless perfection are inseparable aspects of Brahman, and that because of this unity the fullest, most complete expression of freedom lies in the active participation of absolute consciousness in the unlimited joy of creation.[1] In order to justify this reinterpretation of Vedānta, Aurobindo, as we would expect, explicitly rejects the Advaitin's radical ontological distinction, the "unbridgeable gulf" between Brahman and the world.[2] Moreover, in Aurobindo's developmental model, as in Hegel's, the transcendence of one level does not entail the cancellation or elimination of that level but its incorporation or integration by that which transcends it.[3] Clearly, then, in the process of reconciling the traditional Advaitic conception of absolute consciousness with an evolutionary perspective, Aurobindo actually modifies the former to the point of giving up its most unique features. Furthermore, while Aurobindo and his disciples try to distance themselves from Hegel,[4] we believe that the two systems share a great number of important similarities and that, indeed, it would not be misleading to call Aurobindo's Integral Philosophy "Indian Hegelianism."

Without minimizing the impact that the developmental conception of consciousness has had on twentieth century thought, how are we to respond to this challenge to the Advaitin's eternally unchanging absolute consciousness ? Clearly, the elevation by Hegel and Aurobindo of the world of form to the level of

---

notes that the evolutionary account of *prakṛti* presented in the Sāṅkhya philosophy is actually much closer to his own evolutionary model than the Western scientific account, although his introduction to the theory of evolution, during his schooling in England, was in terms of the latter.

1. Cf. *The Life Divine*, II., pp. 879-945.

2. *Ibid.*, I., p. 165. In this context, Aurobindo argues that the stages of consciousness, e.g., waking, dream, deep sleep and *turīya*, are all phases or direct expressions of Spirit in man.

3. *Ibid.*, I., pp. 325-326.

4. Cf. *Ibid.*, I., p. 165; Haridas Chaudhuri, *The Philosophy of Integralism* pp. 26, 29, 36, 38.

Spirit renders contingency, chaos and irrationality inexplicable and unreal. Aside from the fact that both Hegel and Aurobindo are led, in the process of trying to justify their respective teleological, evolutionary models, to somewhat fanciful accounts of the significance of certain natural, historical and cultural developments, the real question is whether or not man is evolving spiritually. This issue is made all the more difficult to resolve because the developmentalists and the Advaitin fail to agree on the very notion of spirituality itself. For the former, the increase in individual liberty and the greater freedom of artistic expression found in at least some contemporary societies (in spite of the frightening power of twentieth century totalitarianism to destroy just these advances) might be interpreted as an indication that a new plateau of spiritual development has been attained. The latter, on the other hand, might argue that social and political as well as biological changes are merely phenomenal developments having little to do with true spirituality. In fact, while applauding the advancement of individual liberty in contemporary society, the Advaitin can conceivably bemoan the passing of conventional morality and interpersonal responsibility, as necessary preliminaries to complete spiritual experience, which has accompanied this increased liberty. Is Spirit or absolute consciousness evolving ? We can only respond that this is one of those questions the answer to which reflects, rather than determines, one's basic metaphysical presuppositions and spiritual commitment.

We are thus led to acknowledge, once again, the comprehensiveness, versatility and uniqueness of the Advaitic theory of consciousness. In spite of reducing the world to the level of illusion, the Advaitic analysis of phenomenal consciousness actually anticipates a number of later Western developments and dilemmas, including a theory of intentional perception based on the recognition of, and attempt to avoid, the problems involved in the mind-body split, a discussion of the function of wish-fulfillment and the creativity of consciousness in dream, and an insight into the dynamics of love and devotion. If the Advaitic analysis of phenomenal consciousness nevertheless seems weak in its lack of elaborate treatment of these points, we can only note that Śaṅkara himself, while aware of this criticism, tended to dismiss it. For Śaṅkara, the focus of attention away from phenomenal consciousness is a natural consequence of the fact that the primary purpose of Vedic wisdom, and therefore of Advaita Vedānta, is not the elaboration of individual experience but the elucidation of, and success on the path leading toward, the realization of Brahman.[1] And if this justification seems unsatisfactory to contemporary philosophers, we can only note that this dissatisfaction is itself an indication of just how radical and unique the Advaitin's uncompromising, transcendental spiritual vision is for our age.

1. *B.S.S.B.* Introduction, 1.1.1-4.

BIBLIOGRAPHY

Primary Sources in Advaita Vedānta

Alston, A. J., trans. *The Naiṣkarmya Siddhi of Śrī Sureśvara.* London : Shanti Sadan, 1959.

Chatterjee, Mohini M., trans. *Viveka-cūḍāmani or Crest Jewel of Wisdom of Śrī Śaṁkarācārya.* Adyar : Theosophical Publishing House, 1947.

Citsukha. *Tattva-pradīpikā*, ed. by Pt. R. K. Sastri. Bombay. Nirnayasagar Press, 1931.

Date, Vinayak Hari, trans. *Vedānta Explained, Śaṁkara's Commentary on the Brahma-sūtras.* 2 Vols. Bombay : Bookseller's Publishing Company, 1954.

Devanji, Prahlad Chandrashekhar, trans. *Siddhāntabindu by Madhusūdanasarasvatī : A Commentary on the Daśaślokī of Śaṁkarācārya.* ("Gaekwad's Oriental Series," Vol. LXIV). Baroda : Oriental Institute, 1933.

Hume, R.E., *The Thirteen Principal Upaniṣads.* New York: Oxford University Press, 1971

Jagadānanda, Swami, trans. *Upadeshasāhasri of Śrī Śaṅkarāchārya.* Mylapore, Madras : Sri Ramakrishna Math, 1961.

Jha, Ganganatha, trans. *The Chāndogyopaniṣad* ("A Treatise on Vedānta Philosophy Translated into English with the Commentary of Śaṅkara"). Poona : Oriental Book Agency, 1942.

Karmarkar, Raghunath Damodar, ed. and trans. *Vedāntakalpalatikā by Madusūdana Sarasvatī.* Poona : Bhandarkar Oriental Research Institute, 1962.

Mādhavānanda, Swami, trans. *The Bṛhadāraṇyaka Upaniṣada ; with the Commentary of Śaṅkarāchārya.* Mayavati, Almora, Himalayas : Advaita Ashrama, 1950.

Mahadevan, T. M. P., ed. and trans. *The Pañcadaśī of Bhāratītīrthā-Vidyāraṇya.* Madras : University of Madras, 1969.

———, ed. and trans. *The Saṁbandha-Vārtika of Sureśvarācārya.* Madras : University of Madras, 1958.

Nikhilānanda, Swami, trans. *The Māṇḍūkyopanisad with Gauḍapāda's Kārikā and Śaṅkara's Commentary.* Mysore : Sri Ramakrishna Asrama, 1955.

Nikhilānanda, Swami, trans. *Self-Knowledge : An English Translation of Śaṅkarāchārya's Ātmabodha,* Mylapore, Madras : Sri Ramakrishna Math, 1962.

Sastri, S. Subramanya, and Ayyangar, T. R. Srinivasa, ed. and trans. *The Jīvan-Mukti-Viveka* ("The Path to Liberation-In-This-Life of Śrī Vidyāraṇya.") Madras : The Theosophical Publishing House, [n.d.]

Sastri, S. S. Suryanarayana, trans. *Siddhānta-leśa-saṅgraha.* Madras : University of Madras, 1935.

———, ed. and trans. *Vedāntaparibhāṣā by Dharmarāja Ahdvarin.* Adyar : The Adyar Library, 1942.

Sastri, S. S. Suryanarayana, and Raja, C. Kunhan, ed. and trans. *The Bhāmatī of Vācaspati : on Śaṅkara's Brahmasūtra-bhāṣya* (Catussūtrī). Madras : Theosophical Publishing House, 1933.

Sastri, S. S. Suryanarayana, and Sen, Saileswar, trans. *Vivaraṇa-prameya-saṅgraha.* Madras : The Sri Vidya Press, 1941.

Shastri, Hari Prasad, trans. *Panchadasi : A Treatise on Advaita Metaphysics by Swami Vidyaranya.* London : Shanti Sadan, 1956.

Venkataramiah, D., trans. *The Pañcapādikā of Padmapāda* ("Gaekwad's Oriental Series," Vol. CVII.) Baroda : Oriental Institute, 1948.

Secondary Sources on Advaita Vedānta and Indian Philosophy

Aurobindo, Sri, *The Life Divine.* 2 vols. Calcutta : Arya Publishing House, 1947.

Bhattacharya, C. "The Objects of the Advaitic Transcendental Consciousness," *Philosophical Quarterly* (Amalner), No. 36, 179-187 (1963).

Bhattacharyya, Krishnachandra. *Studies in Philosophy.* 2 vols. Edited by Gopinath Bhattacharyya, Calcutta : Progressive Publishers, 1956.

———, "Subject as Freedom," *Search for the Absolute in neo-Vedānta.* Edited by George Bosworth Burch. Honolulu : University Press of Hawaii, 1976.

Brooks, Richard. "The Meaning of 'Real' in Advaita Vedānta," *Philosophy East and West,* XIX, No. 4, Oct., 1969, pp. 65-78.

Chaudhuri, Haridas. *The Philosophy of Integralism*. Pondicherry: Sri Aurobindo Ashram, 1957.

Chaudhuri, Anil Kumar Ray. *Self and Falsity in Advaita Vedānta*. Calcutta : Progressive Publishers, 1955.

Chaudhury, P. J. "Vedānta as Phenomenology," *Bulletin of the Ramakrishna Mission Institute of Culture* (Calcutta), IX, No. 3, 56-63 (1958).

Chethimattam, John B. *Consciousness and Reality*. Bangalore : Dharmaram College, 1967.

Das Gupta, Krishna. *The Shadow World*. Delhi : Atma Ram, 1971.

Dasgupta, Surendranath. *A History of Indian Philosophy*. 5 vols. Cambridge : Cambridge University Press, 1922-55.

Datta, Dhirendramohan. *Six Ways of Knowing*. London : George Allen and Unwin, 1932.

Deussen, Paul. *The System of the Vedānta*. Translated by Charles Johnston. Chicago : Open Court, 1912.

Deutsch, Eliot. *Advaita Vedānta A Philosophical Reconstruction*. Honolulu : University Press of Hawaii, 1969.

Devaraja, N. K. *Introduction to Śaṅkara's Theory of Knowledge*. Varanasi : Motilal Banarsidass, 1962.

Frauwallner, Erich. *History of Indian Philosophy*. Vol. I. Translated by V. M. Bedekar. Motilal Banarsidass Delhi, 1974.

Guenon, Rene. *Man and His Becoming According to the Vedānta*. Translated by Richard C Nicholson. New York : The Noonday Press, 1958.

Hiriyanna, Mysore. *Popular Essays in Indian Philosophy*. Mysore : Kāvyālaya Publishers, 1952.

Iyer, M. K. Venkatarama. *Advaita Vedānta*. Bombay : Asia Publishing House, 1964.

Kadankavil, Kurian. *The Philosophy of the Absolute*. Bangalore : Dharmaram Publications, 1972.

Kuppuswamy, B. K. "Imagery and the Antaḥkaraṇa Theory of Perception," *Journal of Madras University*, No. 7, 17-23 (1946).

Mahadevan, T. M. P. *Gauḍapāda*. Madras : University of Madras, 1952.

———. *The Philosophy of Advaita*. Madras : Ganesh and Co., 1957.

Malkani, G. R. *Metaphysics of Advaita Vedānta*. Amalner : Indian Institute of Philosophy, 1961.

———. *Vedāntic Epistemology*. Amalner : Indian Institute of Philosophy, 1953.

Marozzi, E. R. "Psychoanalysis and Vedānta," *Essays in Philosophy Presented to Dr T. M. P. Mahadevan*, Madras : 368-375, 1962.

McDermott, Robert A., ed., *The Essential Aurobindo*. New York : Schocken Books, 1973.

Mishra, Umesha. "Dream Theory in Indian Thought," *The Allahabad University Studies*, Vol. 4.

Mukerji, A. C. *The Nature of Self*. Allahabad : The Indian Press, 1943.

Mukherjee, M. "Two Types of Subjectivism in Monistic Vedānta," *Indian Historical Quarterly*, No. 9, 912-922 (1933).

Murty, K. Satchidananda. *Revelation and Reason in Advaita Vedānta*. New York : Columbia University Press, 1961.

Organ, Troy. *The Self in Indian Philosophy*. The Hague : Mouton and Co., 1967.

Otto, Rudolf. *Mysticism East and West*. Translated by R. Payne Bracey. New York : Macmillan 1932.

Puri, Lekh Raj. *Mysticism The Spiritual Path*. 2 vols. Punjab : Radha Soami Satsang Beas, 1964.

Ramanujachari, R. "Vedānta on Freedom and Moral Responsibility," *Journal of Annamalai University*, No. 2, 17-27, 60, 160-172 (1934).

Rao, G. Hanumantha. "The Development of the Advaita Doctrine of Antaḥkaraṇa in Relation to Perception," *Philosophical Quarterly* (Amalner), No. 16, 183-191 (1940-41).

Rao, S. K. Ramachandra. *Development of Psychological Thought in India*. Mysore : Kavyalaya Publishers, 1962.

Rao, T. B. "Dreamless Sleep (Suṣupti) in Vedānta," *Vedānta Kesari* (Madras), No. 32, 97ff. (1945-46).

Roy, S. S. *The Heritage of Śaṅkara*. Allahabad : Udayana Publications, 1965.

Saksena, S. K. *Nature of Consciousness in Hindu Philosophy*. Benares : Nand Kishore and Bros., 1944.

Sastri, Asutosh Bhattacharya. "Different Types and Stages of Emancipation in Śaṅkara's School of Vedānta," *Prabuddha Bharata* (Calcutta) No. 41, 603-5 (1936).

Sastri, Kokilesvar. "How Suṣupti Benefits our Waking State," *Aryan Path* No. 9, 384 ff. (1938).

———, "Our Waking and Dreaming Worlds in Śaṁkara Vedānta," *Kalyana Kalpataru* (Gorakhpur) No. 3, 57-61 (1936).

Sastri, P. S. "Principles of Non-contradiction," *Philosophical Quarterly* (Amalner), No. 30, 233-236 (1958).

Sastry, R. Sama. "Avidya Psychology," *Pathak Commemorative Volume*, Poona : 139-150 (1934).

Satprakasānanda, Swami. *Methods of Knowledge*. London : George Allen and Unwin, 1965.

Sengupta, B. K. "The Concept of Sākṣin as a Unique Advaitic Principle of Knowledge," *Calcutta Review*, No. 140, 231-240 (1956).

Sharma, Baldev Raj. *The Concept of Ātman in the Principal Upaniṣads*. New Delhi : Dinesh Publications, 1972.

Sharma, V. A. *Citsukha's Contribution to Advaita*, Mysore : Kāvyālaya Pub. 1974.

Sinha, Devabrata. "Concept of Sākṣin in Advaita Vedānta," *Our Heritage* No. 2, 325-32 (1954).

———, "Study on the Advaita Theory of Knowledge : The Concept of Self-Illumination," *Calcutta Review*, No. 131, 53-64 (1954).

Sinha, Jadunath. *Indian Psychology—Perception*. London : Kegan Paul, Trench, Trübner, 1934.

Sprung, Mervyn, ed. *The Problem of Two Truths in Buddhism and Vedānta*. Dordrecht : Reidel, 1973.

Staal, J. F. *Advaita and Neo-Platonism : A Critical Study in Comparative Philosophy*. Madras : University of Madras, 1961.

Sundaram, P. K. *Advaita Epistemology with Special Reference to Iṣṭasiddhi*. Madras : University of Madras, 1968.

Thornton, Edward. "Jungian Psychology and the Vedānta," *Aryan Path,* No. 35, 159-63, (1964).

Upadhyaya, Veermani Prasad. *Lights on Vedānta*. ("Chowkhamba Sanskrit Series," Vol. VI). Varanasi : 1959.

Sources in Western Philosophy

Blakney, Raymond Bernard, trans. and ed. *Meister Eckhart*. New York : Harper, 1941.

Campbell, Joseph, ed. *The Portable Jung*. Translated by R. F. C. Hull, New York : Penguin, 1976.

Campbell, Roy, trans. *St. John of the Cross Poems*. Baltimore : Penguin, 1968.

Ellis, W. D. *A Sourcebook of Gestalt Psychology*. New York : Harcourt, Brace and Co., 1939.

Farber, Marvin. *The Aims of Phenomenology*. New York : Harper, 1966.

———. *The Foundation of Phenomenology*. Albany : SUNY Press, 1968.

Freud, Sigmund. *A General Introduction to Psychoanalysis*. Translated by Joan Riviere. Garden City : Garden City Books, 1952.

———. *The Interpretation of Dreams*. Translated by A. A. Brill. New York : The Modern Library, 1950.

———. *New Introductory Lectures on Psychoanalysis*. Translated by James Strachey. New York : Norton, 1965.

Garfield, Patricia. *Creative Dreaming*. New York : Simon and Schuster, 1975.

Gobar, Ash. *Philosophical Foundation of Genetic Psychology and Gestalt Psychology*. The Hague : Martinus Nijhoff, 1968.

Gurwitsch, Aron. *The Field of Consciousness*. Pittsburgh : Duquesne University Press, 1964.

———. *Studies in Phenomenology and Psychology*. Evanston : Northwestern University Press, 1966.

Gustafson, Donald, ed. *Essays in Philosophical Psychology*. Garden City : Anchor Books, 1964.

Haldane, E. S. and Ross, G. T. R., trans. and ed. *The Philosophical Works of Descartes*, Cambridge University Press, 1911-1912.

Hamilton, Edith and Cairns, Huntington, ed. *Plato The Collected Dialogues*. Princeton : Princeton University Press, 1963.

Hume, David. *A Treatise of Human Nature*. Edited by L. A. Selby Bigge. Oxford : 1888.

Husserl, Edmund. *Cartesian Meditations*. Translated by Dorian Cairns. The Hague : Martinus Nijhoff, 1960.

———. *The Crisis of European Sciences and Transcendental Phenomenology*. Translated by David Carr. Evanston : Northwestern University Press, 1970.

———. *Ideas*. Translated by W. R. Boyce Gibson. London : George Allen and Unwin, 1958.

Husserl, Edmund. *Phenomenology and the Crisis of Philosophy : Philosophy as Science and the Crisis of European Man*. Translated by Quentin Lauer. New York : 1965.

Hyppolite, Jean. *Genesis and Structure of Hegel's Phenomenology of Spirit*. Translated by Samuel Cherniak and John Heckman. Evanston : Northwestern University Press, 1974.

James, William. *The Principles of Psychology*. 2 vols. New York : Dover, 1950.

Jung, C. G. *Dreams*. Translated by R. F. C. Hull. Princeton : Princeton University Press, 1972.

———. *Two Essays on Analytical Psychology*. ("The Collected Works of C. G. Jung," Vol. VII.) Translated by R. F. C. Hull. New York : Pantheon, 1952.

Kant, Immanuel. *Critique of Pure Reason*. Translated by Norman Kemp Smith. New York : The Humanities Press, 1933; St. Martin's Press, 1965.

Kavanaugh, K. and Rodriguez, O., trans. *The Collected Works of St. John of the Cross*. Garden City : Doubleday, 1964.

Kaufmann, Walter, trans. and ed. *Hegel Texts and Commentary*. Garden City : Doubleday, 1966.

Kockelmans, Joseph J., ed. *Phenomenology The Philosophy of Edmund Husserl and its Interpretation*. New York : Doubleday, 1967.

———. *Edmund Husserl's Phenomenological Psychology*. Pittsburgh : Duquesne University Press, 1967.

Koffka, Kurt. *Principles of Gestalt Psychology*. London : Routledge and Kegan Paul, 1935.

Kohler, Wolfgang. *Gestalt Psychology : An Introduction to New Concepts in Modern Psychology*. New York : Liveright, 1947.

Lauer, Quentin. *Hegel's Idea of Philosophy*. New York : Fordham University Press, 1974.

———. *Phenomenology : Its Genesis and Prospect*. New York : Harper, 1958.

Locke, John. *Two Treatises of Government*. Edited by Peter Laslett. Cambridge, 1960.

MacDonald, M. "Sleeping and Waking," *Mind*, LXII, 202-215 (1957).

Merleau-Ponty, Maurice. *Phenomenology of Perception*. Translated by Colin Smith. New York : Humanities Press, 1962.

Mure, Geoffrey Reginald Gilchrist. *An Introduction to Hegel*. Oxford : The Clarendon Press, 1940.

Natanson, Maurice. *Edmund Husserl Philosopher of Infinite Tasks*. Evanston : Northwestern University Press, 1973.

———. "Phenomenology and Existentialism : Husserl and Sartre on Intentionality," *Philosophy Today*. No. 3. Edited by Jerry H. Gill. New York : Macmillan, 1970.

Otto, Rudolph. *Mysticism East and West*. New York : Macmillan, 1932.

Piaget, Jean. *The Child's Conception of Physical Causality*. Translated by M. Gabain. Patterson, New Jersey : Littlefield, Adams and Co., 1960.

———. *The Child's Conception of Time*. Translated by A. J. Pomerans. New York : Basic Books, 1970.

———. *Insights and Illusions of Philosophy*. Translated by Wolfe Mays. New York : The World Publishing Co., 1974.

Piaget, Jean and Inhelder, B. *The Child's Conception of Space*. Translated by F. J. Langdon and J. L. Lunzer. London : Routledge and Paul, 1956.

Sarlemijn, Andries. *Hegel's Dialectic*. Translated by Peter Kirschenmann. Dordrecht : Reidel, 1975.

Sartre, Jean-Paul. *The Transcendence of the Ego*. Translated with Introduction by Robert Kirkpatrick and Forrest Williams. New York : Farrar, Straus and Co., 1964.

Schumacher, E. F. *Small is Beautiful* : New York : Harper & Row, 1973.

Shrader, George Alfred Jr., ed. *Existential Philosophers: Kierkegaard to Merleau-Ponty*. New York: McGraw-Hill, 167

Spencer, Sidney. *Mysticism in World Religion*. Baltimore: Penguin, 1963.

Spiegelberg, Herbert. *The Phenomenological Movement*. 2 vols. The Hague : Martinus Nijhoff, 1965.

Stace, Walter T. *Mysticism and Philosophy*. Philadelphia : Lippincott, 1960.

Straus, Erwin. *The Primary World of Senses*. Glencoe : The Free Press, 1963.

Underhill, Evelyn. *Mysticism*, New York : Dutton, 1948.

Zaehner, Robert C. *Concordant Discord*. Oxford : Oxford University Press, 1970.

———. *Hindu and Muslim Mysticism*. London : University of London Press, 1960.

———. *Mysticism Sacred and Profane*. Oxford : Oxford University Press, 1957.

INDEX